the Castle

Dorothy Hamilton

Illustrated by Esther Rose Graber

For Jamiey a special
friend and an appreciated
reader
By Dorothy Hamilton
Dec. 14, 1976

HERALD PRESS
Scottdale, Pennsylvania
Kitchener, Ontario
1975

Library of Congress Cataloging in Publication Data

Hamilton, Dorothy, 1906-
   The castle.

   SUMMARY: Teen-age Carol befriends the lonely daughter
of the richest man in town, whose family has lots of
money but little pleasure in life.
   [1. Friendship — Fiction. 2. Christian life — Fic-
tion] I. Graber, Esther Rose. II. Title.
PZ7.H18136Cas   [Fic]   75-15599
ISBN 0-8361-1775-1
ISBN 0-8361-1776-X pbk.

THE CASTLE
Copyright © 1975 by Herald Press, Scottdale PA 15683
   Published simultaneously in Canada by Herald Press,
   Kitchener, ON N2G 1A7
Library of Congress Catalog Card Number: 75-15599
International Standard Book Numbers:
   0-8361-1775-1   (hardcover)
   0-8361-1776-X   (softcover)
Printed in the United States of America
Design by Alice B. Shetler

the Castle

To Frances Casey

1

For the first time in her life, at least for as far back as she could remember, Carol Retherford didn't envy Veronica Kingsbury. "All these years I've dreamed about how it would be to live in *The Castle*. But now . . . now that I really know Nicky . . . I feel a little sorry for her."

Carol was late getting home from school because she'd stopped to help out in her father's shoe store. A lot of people didn't think of buying boots until the ground was covered with snow. Icy pellets stung Carol's cheeks as she stopped across the street from the entrance of the Kingsbury estate. She pulled the shawl collar of her red corduroy coat up around her face. She watched a flicker of light grow into a golden glow in the milky glass globes which were anchored in iron on top of the stone gateposts.

These lamps were in line with the windows in Carol's room and she loved to lie in bed and go to sleep looking at their misty light. She glanced up the hill before turning to go around the house on the curving flagstone walk. Lights glowed in only two of the windows in the mansion which people of Winchester had called Kingsbury Castle for more than forty years. Carol knew that one of these windows was in the wide entrance hall and the other in Veronica's room. *And that's sort of fantastic! Four weeks ago I didn't even know which room was Nicky's. And we've lived across the street from each other all our lives.*

It didn't seem strange to Carol that she'd never been in Nicky's room in those fourteen years. What surprised her was that things had changed and that she and Veronica were friends. Very few Winchester people had been invited to *The Castle.* The spiked iron gates were mostly opened for cars with license plates from other counties and states and for trucks making deliveries. The clanging gates seemed to separate the Kingsburys from the town they'd built.

As Carol hurried around to the back door she remembered something her father had said a few weeks ago. "It's a wonder to me that Arthur, Jr., hasn't built a moat."

"A moat?" Carol's mother said. "What ever. . . ."

"*And* a drawbridge. To keep that youngest girl of his . . . what's her name?"

"Veronica," Carol said.

"I knew it was something fancy," Mr. Retherford

8

said. "Like the other one who eloped."

"Alexandra," Carol's mother said. "But why this sudden interest in the Kingsburys? You've prided yourself on being one of the few people who doesn't gossip about their comings and goings."

"True," Carol's father said. "I've always figured that if they don't want to have anything to do with us I can manage to leave *them* alone. But I caught a glimpse of that younger girl's face tonight. The limousine was pulling in the driveway as I came home. She looked sad . . . lonely."

"She probably is," Carol's mother said. "Her brothers are married and although her sister lives here in town, people say she isn't allowed to come home. What's the name of the boy she married?"

"Weaver. Corby Weaver," Carol's father said. "He runs the filling station out on the junction with the highway. Fine young man. Arthur, Jr., can't see the forest for the trees."

"Whatever that means!" Carol's mother said. "I fail to see how that saying fits the situation."

"I don't know that it does. I'm ready to end this conversation."

Carol thought several times of what her father had said about Veronica looking sad. She watched for her at school and mentally debated whether or not she should try to be friendly. *I don't know if she wants friends. But then, I don't know that she doesn't.*

Again she wondered why Mr. Kingsbury didn't send Veronica to a boarding school. *Looks like that's what he'd do since he doesn't want his family to associate with people in Winchester.*

Carol and anyone who'd lived in the town for more

than a year knew that the history of the place and the Kingsburys went back for the same length of time. Arthur Senior had located his glass factory at Winchester when it was only a village, a ticktacktoe, with two short streets crossing two going in the other direction. He built *The Castle* soon after the first of several factory buildings was finished. The house was then a mile away from town. Now Winchester surrounded the fenced-in block which was centered by the white brick mansion.

Knowing all this history didn't help Carol understand why the founding family kept away from people in town. The first glint of understanding came that afternoon four weeks ago. Classes were over for the day. Carol and Betty Rose Saunders were walking toward their lockers. They met and passed Cleo Moore, who stopped and called back, "Is it still okay if I come over tonight?"

"Certainly," Carol said. She turned and saw Veronica. She was at her locker, fastening the blue silk loop on her creamy fur coat.

"Do you do that a lot?" Veronica asked. "Visit each other?"

"Well, yes," Carol said. She started to ask why. Then she saw the look in Veronica's eyes. *She is sad.*

"I didn't mean to be nosy," Veronica said.

"You weren't," Carol replied. "But I'm sort of surprised that you asked . . . or wanted to talk."

"I've wanted to, many times. But . . . well it's not easy for me to be friendly, mainly because I'm not supposed to be."

"Because of your father?"

"You know? Does everyone talk about us like that?"

"Yes, they do. But not in a mean way. They know your father doesn't want his family to associate with anyone here. That's not hard to see."

"Could we walk home together?" Veronica said.

"Certainly," Carol said. "But you always ride."

"I know, but the car's in the garage, and Daddy and Mother are out of town. Flora said she'd call a taxi, but I begged to walk."

"Flora? Is she your cook?"

"Yes and housekeeper and a kind of lifesaver to mother and me, especially since Alexandra got married."

The two girls went out the side door and walked slowly along Main Street and then down slanting Randolph Avenue. Veronica seemed to be bubbling over with questions. She wanted to know if Carol and her friends did homework together, or made fudge like girls in books, or talked all night.

"That sounds like stories I've read about colleges and boarding schools," Carol said. "And that brings up a question I've had in my mind. If you don't want to answer just tell me it's none of my business. I won't get mad."

"Go ahead."

"Well, if your father wants to keep you away from us *why* does he send you to school here?"

"Not to boarding school, you mean?"

"Right."

"That's easy to answer. It's my grandfather's wish. He made a lot of money here and sort of thought of himself as the Lord of Winchester. Like he made the town."

"My father says he did, almost."

"Well, anyway, Grandfather thought that Kingsburys should live in their town and go to its schools. Mother said he felt a ruling class couldn't rule if it was absent."

"He really thought of himself as a kind of ruler?"

"I'm afraid so," Veronica said. "And Daddy's a lot like him now. He didn't used to be so strict until Alexandra ran away with Corby. Since then I feel like I live behind bars. He's afraid I'll do the same."

"I can see why he'd try to keep you from going with boys," Carol said. "But how about girl friends? Why doesn't he approve of us?"

"Because you could introduce me to boys, or I could meet them at your homes."

"That doesn't seem too realistic to me," Carol said. "You see boys at school all the time. And I'm sure they see you."

"I know. Papa's not always reasonable, not since Alexandra left. He's moody and withdrawn. Mother's worried."

As they came to *The Castle* gates, Carol said, "Would you ever disobey him? Like by coming to see me?"

"Not if he specifically said not to see you. But he probably doesn't even know you live over there. And even then I'd ask Mother first. I'd not want to deceive her."

"Will you? Ask her, I mean."

"Yes, I will. When she gets home."

"Good! Maybe we could do some of those things you mentioned, like make fudge. But our get-togethers are not all fun. Most of the time we just do homework."

2

Carol hurried home with the conversation with Veronica bubbling in her mind. She could hardly wait to tell her mother and called, "Guess what happened!" as she crossed the back porch. But no one was at home. She read the note on the kitchen table: "At church. Help needed."

"Who's help?" Carol wondered, "Mother's or mine? And for what?"

She decided to find the answers to her questions after she'd changed clothes and eaten a peanut butter and brown sugar sandwich. The sun was almost down by the time she crossed the church parking lot. The gray-blue sky was streaked with orange. Seven cars stood in the lanes which were marked by yellow diagonal lines. What could so many be doing this time of day?

Her steps on the concrete stairs did not muffle the whirring sound of sewing machines. For several minutes no one noticed that she was in the brightly lighted basement. Heads were bent over the cloth being fed under dancing needles. Two ladies were guiding scissors around tissue paper patterns.

"Want a job?" someone said from behind Carol. She turned to see Mrs. Trent, who was carrying a tray of Saran-wrapped sandwiches.

"What's going on?" Carol asked.

"Come over to the counter while I pour hot chocolate and I'll tell you," Mrs. Trent said.

Carol put sandwiches and napkins on paper plates while the lady with silver white hair told her about a near-tragedy. "Two of the migrant families had gone back to Texas, but a hurricane had destroyed almost all of their hometown. They headed back to Indiana hoping to find work. The camp outside of town was closed and the owner is in Florida," Mrs. Trent said. "But a farmer gave them permission to stay in a run-down tenant house. It burned to the ground this morning."

"Was anyone hurt?" Carol asked.

"No. The men were looking for jobs and the mothers had taken the small children to the woods to gather fallen limbs and branches for fuel."

"And now you're sewing for these families?"

"Yes. Our outreach fund is too low to buy ready-made clothes *and* rent a house. So we've measured everyone and are trying to get one change of clothing for each of them before this day's over."

Carol knew about the church outreach program. Everyone helped in one way or another. Her Sunday school class sold Scripture Christmas cards every year to add to the fund.

As she served the workers she saw her mother come from the stairway. She came up to Carol and said, "I barely made it before the stores closed. We needed bias tape and red and white rickrack."

"Want me to help there, or go home and get supper?"

"Well, we're fairly well organized here. So helping at home seems best. I'll be there . . . but I can't say when."

Carol felt a little let down as she walked home. The excitement of getting to know Veronica was ebbing. Her thoughts went back in time as she walked. She recalled the Easter egg hunts the Kingsburys held for Winchester children every year. This was the only time when the scrolled iron gates swung open for them, but the doors of *The Castle* remained closed.

These hunts were held every year until the spring Alexandra eloped with Corby. Carol remembered how she looked forward to running around the sloping front lawn. She recalled that every child was given a special favor besides the foil-wrapped eggs and marshmallow chickens. Carol's favorite was a porcelain egg encrusted with pale violets. Another year it was domed paperweights in which a white rabbit was showered with snowflakes.

One thing was always the same. The cook brought trays of chocolate eclairs to the back terrace. Sometimes the creamy icing was still warm, so Carol knew the pastries had been made in the Kingsbury kitchen.

15

She'd bought a few éclairs in the town bakery, but they weren't the same.

The next day Carol had a chance to tell Veronica what she'd remembered. She nearly bumped into her at the cafeteria door. "You eating *here*?"

"Yes," Veronica said. "Mama's car is not running and in a way I'm glad."

"Well come on," Carol said. As they set their salmon croquettes, creamed peas, and crumb pudding on the table," she added, "The pudding looks good but it can't compare to the éclairs we used to have at your Easter egg hunts."

"I remember those times," Veronica said. "But they weren't really mine. I had to watch."

"I know," Carol said. "I always saw you, usually from a certain upstairs window."

"That was my room. I enjoyed the egg hunts anyway," Veronica said, "even if I was only looking on. But like in a lot of other ways, life changed for Mother and I after Alexandra married Corby. Mainly Daddy. He's different. It's like . . . like he's in a shell. And has pulled us in with him."

"Your brothers are married, aren't they?" Carol asked.

"Yes. Before Alex left. It doesn't bother them much. But it's different for Mother and me."

"Don't you see Alexandra anymore?" Carol asked.

"Oh, yes. We go there. Daddy can't stop that and he knows it. And we have such fun. Especially since the baby came. We call him the Little Weaver. He sorts of weaves two families together . . . all except Daddy."

"Does your father expect you to live apart for-

16

ever? Or shouldn't I ask?" Carol said.

"Probably not," Veronica said. She told Carol that she'd gone out with sons of some of her father's business associates, boys from other towns. "But it's not been much fun with anyone. Especially not since I met Bruce."

Within a few minutes the cafeteria was full of people hunting seats. Cleo and Betty Rose sat down across and a few chairs down from Carol. They looked surprised to see her with Veronica. Sally Blane went further. She stopped near Veronica's chair and said to someone, "My! My! We're being treated to a visit from royalty. A real state occasion!"

Veronica pretended not to hear and kept on eating, but the pink in her cheeks deepened to a flush. Carol couldn't follow her example. She knew Sally. Being ignored made Sally more determined to be noticed. "It's a custom here," Carol said, "that Winchester students eat in the cafeteria when they choose. Or hadn't you heard?"

Sally evidently couldn't think of an answer so she flounced away, her high heels clicking on the tile floor.

"Don't pay any attention to her," Carol said. "None of us do . . . any more than we can help. I'm curious. Who's Bruce?"

"Could we go somewhere and talk, even if there's not much to say on that subject? Probably never will be."

"Let me finish this crumb pudding," Carol said. "It's too good to leave."

They wandered to the balcony of the gym. Two teams of the noon league were playing basketball.

The two girls talked as balls thumped, whistles blew, and feet pounded up and down the hardwood floor.

Veronica didn't say much about Bruce Harrison — just that he was a freshman at the university and worked part time for the landscaping firm that took care of the Kingsbury grounds.

"I talked to him a few times, but not about anything personal. Like saying we had box-elder bugs and that the lawn mower blade needed to be sharpened."

"No," Carol said, "I wouldn't call that a romantic conversation. But you do like him, don't you?"

"Sort of. He's handsome and serious . . . at least that's how he seems. I'll probably never get a chance to find out if I'm right or wrong. Daddy won't ever let me date him, I know."

"I'm in the same boat in a way."

"You mean *you* don't go out with boys?"

"No. My mother and father say not until I'm a junior."

"Does that bother you?"

"No, not really. The only time it does is when some of the girls call me odd or square or whatever word they're using at the time."

"Do all the girls in our class date?" Veronica asked.

"A lot do. But not everyone. Not Cleo or Betty Rose. A few others aren't particularly in a big rush to grow up either. Mom says there'll be plenty of time for boys later."

3

The warning signal buzzed from somewhere over-head. "Five minutes to get to the second floor . . . and at the far end of the hall," Veronica said.

"I just now realized," Carol said. "I don't know what you're taking."

"Whatever my father thinks will get me to Radcliffe. It's French this hour."

"Is that where you want to go?"

Veronica shrugged her shoulders. "How do I know? I'm not even sure I want to go to college. So far no one's asked *me*."

The girls stopped at the top of the ramp. "Before I go," Veronica said, "I've been wanting to ask you about your nickname."

"My nickname?"

"Yes. I heard Sally call you Carrie."

"Oh, that one. She's the only one who does. The others don't because they know I hate it. And that's exactly why Sally uses it."

"Do you have another?"

"Some people — those who know me best — call me Songbird, which I'm not. They use it because I'm Carol. Why did you want to know? Do you have a nickname?"

"No. But it seems nice — warm and friendly."

"What would you like to be called?"

"Do people nickname themselves?" Veronica asked.

"No. I guess not. I know no one would call me Carrie if that's the way it worked. I have to run. I'll think on it. Meet me at the lockers."

"I'll be there."

Snowflakes were sifting from the misty gray sky when the girls walked out of the school building. The maroon convertible was waiting along the curb. "Oh, it's fixed already," Veronica said. "I'll run over and see if I can coax Flora to let me walk home with you."

When she came toward Carol, she was smiling, "It's okay. Flora doesn't like making such decisions. She's a little afraid of my father. I truly think it was what you said about her éclairs that helped her make up her mind to say yes. I told her last night."

As they crossed the business district, Carol said, "I've been thinking. How would you like for me to call you Nicky? Or . . . it *could* be Ronnie . . . or Vernie . . . but I don't like that last one."

"Which do you like?"

"Nicky. It fits."

"Well, fine. I'm Nicky . . . to you anyway."

The girls didn't hurry. They walked slowly and words of one seemed to tumble out and bump into those of the other. Neither seemed to want the walk to end. They paused to look in windows as they crossed town. Veronica stopped in the middle of one block and walked back a few steps. "I didn't know there was a bookstore in Winchester," she said.

"It's been here a long time," Carol answered. "But they never really have many books, mostly stationery and gifts."

"Could we go in?"

"Sure. I have lots of time. Now I wouldn't spend money on some things in here. But there's a selection."

By the time they headed toward home, dark clouds were tumbling overhead. "Nights like this I think of the gardener's cottage." Veronica said.

"You mean that little house in the back corner?"

"You've seen it?"

"A little of it," Carol said. "We've peeked through the iron fence. But I don't understand why . . . how . . . ?"

"Oh, it's sort of a playhouse, or a pretend home to me. In-between times when no one lived in it we played down there, Alexandra and I. And the boys sometimes. Then after I outgrew that, I used it for a retreat. A place to read, or think, or cry."

"I had a place like that," Carol said. "Only it wasn't a house. It was a place on my grandfather's farm, under a weeping willow tree. I loved to sit in the cool shade and pretend the branches were green lace curtains."

"Did you think about it when you weren't there?"

"Oh, yes," Carol said. "I did and do. Especially when I'm tired or upset about something."

"That's how I am about the cottage. I pretend I'm living in it. I've chosen furniture . . . in my mind . . . even white ruffly curtains and a copper teakettle and a high-backed rocking chair."

"I wonder why we do this?" Carol asked.

"Oh, I don't know," Veronica said. "Unless we're wanting to feel safe."

"Or to be in the secret place of the Most High," Carol said softly.

"That sounds like the Bible. Do you go to church?"

"Yes," Carol said. She wanted to ask if the Kingsburys went but if they didn't, Nicky might think she was judging.

The girls hadn't paid attention to where they were. Veronica looked at her watch and said, "It's past four. Daddy comes home early sometimes. I'd better get up to the house. See you, and thanks."

"For what?"

"For more than you know," Nicky said. "Goodbye."

"She didn't say it was time for her to go home," Carol thought. "Just up to the house." This thought made her feel grateful to be headed for the warmth of her own home.

Her mother was ironing in the kitchen. "I'm way behind with my work," she said. "Being at church yesterday and most of this morning put kinks in my schedule."

"Did you get the sewing done?"

"For now. For that one family. Would you take an

armload of clothes upstairs? It's about time for me to start supper."

"I will in a minute," Carol said. "And I'll hurry back to help cook. But I've been bursting to tell you something for nearly two days."

"Then tell me."

"You're never going to believe who I walked home with tonight and yesterday. And ate lunch with."

"I'll believe you. Why wouldn't I?"

"Because. It was Veronica Kingsbury."

Carol watched her mother's face. She didn't even look up, or arch her eyebrows. She just kept on nudging the iron around the ruffles on that pink blouse.

After a minute of waiting, Carol said, "You don't act surprised."

"Well, it seems natural to me. You live across the street from each other and go to the same school. Being a year older doesn't mean that she wouldn't want to associate with you."

"Mother! You *know* how it's always been. Being a Kingsbury's why she hasn't ever been friendly."

"That's what's unnatural," Carol's mother said. "I always have thought so. Of course I couldn't know how Veronica felt. She could have preferred to stay apart, simply because that's the way it's always been."

"She didn't prefer it . . . or like it," Carol said. "Daddy was right when he said she looked sad and lonely."

After supper the telephone rang and Carol was surprised to hear Nicky's voice. "I just called my sister. We're going over there for a while. And I thought it would be fun to call you."

"It is. You know something, I don't even know your number."

"It's unlisted. Grab a pencil. Write 468-7739. Oh, here's Mother already. I'll tell you tomorrow why we're going to Alexandra's. It's special."

4

Carol didn't see Veronica until she went to her locker at the close of school the next day. But she did find a note in the crack of the door at noon. "Have to eat at home today. Daddy's bringing someone out to lunch. Could you walk home with me this evening?"

When Carol took her tray to the usual table she noticed that Sally Blane was sitting with Cleo and Betty Rose. *This* wasn't usual. These three girls had never been close friends, not in grade school nor here in Kingsbury High. Sally was what Nancy Retherford called "a floater." She didn't have any close relationships with anyone.

Maybe that's because of the way she talks about

everyone, Carol thought as she took her tray three chairs down from the group. *Like I'm almost sure she's talking about me now.*

Betty Rose looked toward Carol where she heard the clink of silverware on the table. Her face flushed as their eyes met. She waved, then looked away.

A strange feeling came over Carol as she buttered her roll. She wasn't used to feeling that she was the subject of conversation between Sally and her good friends. Everyone knew that Sally jabbered jealously about everyone. *But now the others seem to be chiming in.*

The tables around Carol were soon filled and she was glad not to be able to see what her friends were doing. But her mind kept running back to one question, *What is Sally saying?*

Before she left the cafeteria she knew the answer. Betty Rose brought her tray to the window of the school kitchen as Carol turned to leave.

"Could I talk to you?" Betty Rose asked.

"If you want," Carol said.

"I want to. But it's not easy to say what I'm thinking or feeling."

Carol looked at her friend and saw that a misty film was clouding her blue eyes. "Come on, let's find an empty classroom."

The two girls threaded their way around groups of sauntering, chattering students until they came to the reading lab. "No one's in here," Carol said.

"No. They wouldn't be unless they were sent," Betty Rose said. "At least that's the way the remedial classes make some kids feel. Like they are stupid or worse."

26

I'm almost sure Sally is talking about me now,
Carol thought as she headed for her usual table.

"I know," Carol said. "I was a student helper last term."

The girls walked to a window which overlooked the tennis courts. They were covered with snow and the nets had been taken down. Boot prints and dog tracks made a jumbled pattern on the snow.

"What's the matter . . . between us?" Carol asked. "Have I done something to hurt you . . . or Clea?"

Betty Rose looked down but she kept tracing circles on the steamy glass. "Yes, in a way. Lately. Well, I might as well say it! You've turned against your old friends and taken up with Veronica Kingsbury."

Carol caught herself rubbing one ear lobe . . . her uneasy mannerism. *I should have known that Sally would make something out of this.*

"I don't think I've turned against anyone," Carol said. "I never thought of doing such a thing."

"But you've walked home with Veronica twice," Betty Rose said. "And you rushed to eat with her when she condescends to associate with us common people."

"Oh, Betty. That doesn't sound like you. Not that last remark. That's Sally's kind of talk," Carol said.

"Maybe so," Betty said. "But you *have* ignored us."

Carol looked back over the past two days. "Have I even once not met you when we planned or refused to go anyplace you asked?"

"Well, no," Betty Rose said. "But it could be we didn't ask because you seemed so busy."

"Is that true?" Carol asked.

"No. I guess not . . . not with me," Betty Rose said. "But Cleo said she was going to call and ask you over to hear her new records. The party line was busy. You were talking to Veronica!"

"Well, sure! For about three minutes. And what's so wrong about that? Clea didn't call back, did she?"

"No. She said you probably didn't have time for her," Betty Rose said.

Suddenly Carol felt impatient. Not with Betty Rose personally. But the pettiness and jealousy seemed so childish. She searched for words, the right kind.

"I like Veronica. You would too if you knew her. And she'd like you. Besides, she's *so* lonely."

"Lonely?" Betty said. "That couldn't be! Cars are always going in and out of The Castle grounds."

"I know," Carol said. "But who's in them? Men. Friends of her father. Repairmen. Salesmen, maybe. But not people her own age. Not even her sister."

"I guess you're right," Betty Rose admitted. "I just didn't think. I guess I've been letting Sally do that for me."

Carol looked at her watch. "The bell for the next class will be ringing in about three minutes. I'd better head upstairs. But why don't you come to my locker at 3:15? I'm meeting Veronica. We're walking home together."

"I wish I *could*," Betty Rose said. "But Future Homemakers Club meets after school. And we're making plans for our bake sale."

"You sure you're not making excuses?" Carol asked.

"I'm sure," Betty Rose said. "Ask me again and I'll prove it."

"Will do!" Carol said as she hurried toward the ramp.

Carol told Veronica that Betty Rose had wanted to walk home with them. But that's all. She didn't want

Nicky to hear what Sally was saying.

"That would have been nice," Veronica said. "Betty's so pretty. I always think of gardenias when I see her lovely skin. Blushing gardenias."

"You're right!" Carol said. "She does have that look." The girls were halfway across the business section of Main Street when Carol asked, "Are you in a big hurry to get home?"

"No. But I'd better call Flora if I'm not to be there by four. Mother's away. Why?"

"Well, I thought we might stop for a Coke or milkshake at the Candy Cave."

"The what?" Veronica said. "Oh, I know! That's the store on the corner with the marble soda fountain. I've seen it as we passed. The fixtures shine in the sunlight."

"You've never been inside?" Carol asked.

"No," Veronica said.

It seemed incredible that anyone, even a Kingsbury, could live in Winchester all her life and not go inside the Candy Cave. It was an institution, a little like the courthouse and Goodrich Park and the statue of Civil War soldiers in the middle of the square.

Carol had sipped strawberry sodas in the confectionery store when her legs were too short to reach the floor from the seat of the wire-backed chairs. She bought Mary Jane caramels and red-hots with pennies. Once she'd saved for weeks to buy a heart-shaped box of candy for her mother's February birthday.

She led the way to a round table in the back of the store. Several kids spoke to her and she introduced Veronica to the people at the tables next to them.

As they sipped their frothy milkshakes Carol said, "You said last night that you'd tell me about your visit at Alexandra's."

"Oh, yes. I want to. Actually it's the reason for going that's news. Mother's going to work."

"Work?" Carol was amazed. Why? Where?"

"At the hospital over in Fort Wayne. She was a nurse."

Carol wasn't exactly surprised to hear that Mrs. Kingsbury was a nurse. "Haven't I heard something about that?" she couldn't help asking. "What does your father think about . . . about her working? Or does he know?"

"He knows and he's opposed, violently at first. Now he's giving her the pouting treatment . . . not talking at all. But before he entered his silent world he said he'd see that she wasn't hired locally."

"Why?" Carol started to ask.

"Because of pride. I think he would've tried to keep her from going anywhere. But not even Daddy could help but see how sad and lonely Mother's been since Alexandra left home. The bitterness is depressing her."

"It's a long drive to Fort Wayne," Carol said.

"I know. But she's only going to be on duty two days a week. That's why we went to see Alexandra. To tell. She's glad Mother is excited about something. It's bothered her that her marriage has caused Daddy to be hard on Mother and me."

"But she's not sorry for her own sake?"

"Oh, no. She's truly happy. And I see why. Partly anyway. Corby's so gentle and such fun. And the baby, he's a sweetheart!"

"Did you have a chance to ask your mother if you could visit me? If it would cause trouble?"

"I didn't tell you? Oh my goodness! I guess being at the Cave drove the subject out of my mind. Yes, I can come. When Daddy's out of town."

She told Carol that her mother hadn't hesitated about giving her permission. "She doesn't like doing things behind Daddy's back, though. And I actually can't understand why she's afraid to stand up to him. But I'm sure she has a reason that seems good to her. And . . . I don't want to make things harder for her. So! I go along with things as they are."

5

As Carol approached the back door of her home she wondered what she'd do that evening. Her parents were scheduled to go with a visitation team from the church which was trying to include others in the fellowship. "Mother doesn't like me to stay alone. Says that immature adults make life unsafe for us dependable teenagers."

I think I'll go over to Mrs. Trent's. If she's not busy, Carol thought. *Or if she's not on a visiting team.*

Something told Carol that her mother was gone before she opened the door. She had an empty feeling. The house seemed lonely. *Maybe that's because Mother's almost always here when school's out. Says she'd miss too much of my childhood if she went gadding about. And I'd miss sharing with her. Like telling her what Nicky said.*

She walked into the kitchen and found the note in its usual place under the peach luster teapot on the shelf above the sink. "At the store. A heavy snow is forecast. We're having another rush of boot buying."

"That probably means Mrs. Trent's busy until closing time. Daddy calls her when there's a lot of business even on her day off."

Carol wasn't ready to do homework, so she called the store and asked what she should do about starting supper.

"We won't have much time," her mother said. "So I've ordered pizzas. We'll pick them up on the way home."

"Is Mrs. Trent working?"

"Yes, why?"

"Oh, I was thinking about going over to see her."

"I'm sorry. But her team's making calls tonight too. We'll talk about plans for you when we get there."

"Say, Mother. Are you *sure* we're going to get more snow?"

"I'm sure," her mother said. "Look out the window."

Carol saw a curtain of snow falling through the air. There was no wind and the large flakes sifted almost straight down. The ground was already covered and the clothesline posts wore fluffy white caps. *That came in a hurry,* Carol thought. *And it's getting dark so early.*

She felt a little restless and didn't know what to do

with herself. The house seemed to be full of echoes and shadows, even after she flicked the switch on two lamps.

She turned the knob on the television set but neither the troubles of the people in the serials nor the cartoons interested her. She'd decided to do her homework when the telephone rang.

"Carol," Veronica said. "Are you doing anything special tonight?"

"No. I've made no promises nor plans. Why?"

"Well, Mother suggested that I call and ask you to stay all night with me. Could you? Would you?"

"I'd love that," Carol said. "I'll have to call my mother at the store. . . . And I have to know this. How about your father?"

"He's in Chicago for two days. Mother came home from Ft. Wayne early because of the weather forecast. And we thought it would be fun to have company."

Carol's mother gave her permission to go and cautioned her to dress in warm clothes and wear high-topped boots. "You may have to wade drifts in the morning. What are you going to eat?"

"Tomato soup and toast," Carol said. "It's that kind of evening."

As Carol crossed the street, she thought. *The globes on the lampposts look like golden moons in the darkness, moons hanging low over Winchester.* Long shadows of the Lombardy Poplar and Blue Spruce trees slanted across the snow-covered lawn. She could see the double doors of *The Castle* in the light of the wrought iron lanterns on either side.

Nicky opened the door before the sound of the

35

chimes faded. "Hi. Come in. We're back in the library where there's a log fire."

Joanne Kingsbury came down the wide hall. She smiled and touched Carol's wrist. "You look like your mother. The same cornflower blue eyes."

Again Carol felt that there was a reason for Mrs. Kingsbury knowing about her mother's eyes. *What is it? What have I heard or partly heard?"*

"Come on back to the library," Nicky said, "and see what Flora's made."

"I don't have to see. I can guess," Carol said. "Chocolate éclairs." She couldn't keep from glancing into the rooms they passed. She caught glimpses of deep chairs covered in deep gold and forest green. Was the upholstery real velvet? Paintings lined the hall on both sides and a high-backed chair sat under each. The frames of the pictures were dull gold and the plush seats of the chairs were tufted rose.

"This is Flora," Joanne Kingsbury said. "We're taking care of her tonight."

"I remember you," Carol said. "Are you hurt? Well, I guess that's a silly question. Your ankle's bandaged."

Flora smiled and nodded. "I twisted my foot coming down the stairs. So I reckon I'll let myself be waited on, as much as I'd rather be up and doing."

"Then how'd you make the éclairs?"

"Oh, they were finished before the swelling started."

"What she means is she didn't tell us she'd been hurt until her walk became a hobble," Veronica's mother said.

The three talked for half an hour. The fingers of flame curled around the stack of logs, sparks darted

36

As Carol walked through The Castle *she saw richly upholstered chairs and walls lined with paintings.*

into the air and flickered out, and fiery coals glowed on the grate. The room was warm and cozy, with it's book-lined walls and soft brown couches and bitter-sweet chairs.

Veronica looked at the crystal and gold clock on the stone mantel and walked to the window. "It's still snowing. Do you think it's too deep for me to show Carol the cottage?"

"I doubt it," her mother said. "The wind's not blowing yet, but it's predicted for later in the evening. Turn on the lights up here."

Carol was willing to go with Nicky, but she could not help wondering why Nicky wanted to show her the gardener's house at night. "Let's go out the front door," Veronica said. "Mother shoveled a path around to the back. It may be partly filled by now, though."

"Your mother shoveled snow?"

"Yes. She loves being out in it. But she has to slip out to do such work."

"Isn't she well? I mean is there some reason . . .?"

"Oh, no. She's fine, except for being depressed some of the time. But Daddy . . . well I guess he thinks we should be like the lady in the nursery rhyme, sit on a cushion and sew a fine seam, which would be very dull."

The girls followed the path to the curving drive which led to the four-car garage. "From here we'll have to make our own tracks," Veronica said.

They passed a sunken garden and a greenhouse. The lights within the octagonal glass building made it a giant lampshade on a carpet of glistening snow.

Veronica led the way around a two-sided wall of evergreen trees in the southwest corner of the estate.

Then Carol could see the small house made of the same kind of white bricks as *The Castle* on the hill-crest. A light with a small round globe gleamed above a solid door which was painted robin's-egg blue.

Veronica took off her white angora mittens and turned the brass key until the lock clicked. "Enter, my friend, and you shall see," she said, "and hear what I'm dying to tell thee."

"I've noticed that about you before. You talk in rhymes sometimes. Like you did just then!"

6

Veronica flipped the light switch and Carol blinked in the sudden brightness. She saw that they'd entered a small kitchen. A square refrigerator filled one corner and a drop-leaf table with matching white chairs the other. Cabinets and a sink ran along the outside wall under two rectangular windows.

"Come on in here," Veronica said. They walked into a large square room with low ceiling and a half wall fenced in one corner. "Daddy had that partition put in when Calvin was here. That was his bedroom. This saved heating the other two rooms."

"It's warm in here," Carol said.

"Yes. Heat pipes run underground to the greenhouse and on down here. The water's turned on and

40

Daddy doesn't want the pipes to freeze. Actually, I think he still hopes to find a gardener like Calvin. Change bothers him a lot."

"It's homey," Carol said. "No wonder you liked to play here."

"We had to share it with the boys. To them it was a hideout. A lot of times I've wished we could live down here. Mother and I anyway. Flora'd probably think she should take care of Daddy. Of course I'm just daydreaming. And I know it."

Carol walked to the window. She could see part of the iron fence in a stream of light. "Do I see a gate?"

"Yes. That was a private entrance for Calvin, and the others. I used to slip out for short walks."

"That's strange. I've walked all around this square lots of times. I never noticed a gate."

"That's because of the bushes — the Barberry and Mock Orange. They're meant to hide the gate. Let's sit down out in the kitchen. I really brought you down here to tell you what's on my mind. You know already about Bruce. Well, I've seen him several times lately. For a few minutes. Like when he covered the roses for winter and cut dead limbs from trees. He's having a rough time."

Veronica told Carol that Bruce might have to drop out of college. She said that his mother was a widow and that her salary as a secretary wasn't enough for her to help him much. "He might have made it except they raised the dorm fees and it's not easy. He doesn't get to work as many hours in winter."

A glimmer of understanding shone in Carol's mind. "And his problem and this cottage — they're related somehow."

41

"Yes. That's it. That's why I wanted to try my idea out on you. If Bruce could live here even for a few weeks, he could save money and stay in school."

"Would you keep this a secret?" Carol asked. "Let Bruce move in without telling either of your parents?"

"No. I'd have to tell Mother and get her permission. If I didn't there'd be trouble for her if Daddy found out. Besides I doubt if Bruce would come if he had to sneak in. And maybe he won't anyway."

"You haven't said anything to him?"

"No, and I've put off talking to Mother. I hate to upset her, I guess."

Carol drew circles in the dust on the drop-leaf table. "I don't know about *your* mother, Nicky, but mine would be hurt if she thought I was keeping something from her in order to protect her. She'd say that's one thing mothers are for — to listen, and try to help."

"I never thought of it like that," Veronica said. "Things have been strained here. We've sort of got in the habit of keeping secrets from each other."

"Does your sister know about Bruce?" Carol asked.

"A little," Veronica said. "There's not really much to know. Alexandra listens but doesn't try to influence me one way or the other. How do you feel about the idea?"

"Well," Carol said. "It does seem too bad that this cozy building can't be used for a good purpose."

"That's exactly what I think. And I've got to find the time and the courage to talk to Mother about it."

The girls stopped at the greenhouse on the way back to *The Castle*. Nicky picked six carnations for

42

Flora. "These white ones edged in pink are her favorites."

Carol was enchanted with Nicky's room. It was a picture in peach and silver, and white embroidered organdy. "I never saw a chaise lounge before," she said as she ran a finger over a tuft in the peach velvet upholstery.

"I'll tell you something," Veronica said. "They're not very comfortable. I'd like to move this one to the storeroom, but it belonged to Grandmother Kingsbury. She had it redone for me. So! I'm stuck with it, like with almost all the furniture in this house. How about a snack before bedtime?"

The girls made hot chocolate in the big kitchen. It looked like the cooking area of a restaurant to Carol. Rows of copper pans hung above the polished range and there were so many cabinets that she wondered how Flora ever found what she needed.

Coming in from the cold made the girls unusually sleepy. Carol could see one window from the twin bed. She raised up on one elbow. "I can't see the lampposts from here. Nicky doesn't know how it is to go to sleep in their light."

The snow let up during the night and the streets were nearly clear the next morning. "The weatherman was wrong about the wind," Joanne Kingsbury said as she drove the girls to school. "Veronica, I'll meet you out front at noon."

"I could eat in the cafeteria," Veronica said.

"I know. And you may another time. I want to take you downtown on a little shopping trip."

"In Winchester?" Veronica asked.

"In Winchester," Mrs. Kingsbury said. "I have

something in mind. Come back and see us, Carol."

As the girls hurried in out of the cold wind, Carol said, "You sounded surprised. That you're going to shop here in Winchester."

"We don't very often," Veronica said. "And almost never in person. Sometimes the owner of Jo's shop sends things up for approval. But mostly we go to Indianapolis or have things made."

"You don't like that?" Carol said.

"Not the part about having things made. Our dressmaker comes over from Union City. My grandmother had her. She's great at needlework. But she sticks pretty close to her old patterns. Sometimes I think she's not been out where people are for years."

As Carol went on to class she could see what Nicky meant. For years every girl in Winchester had envied Nicky because of her clothes. They'd begged for velvet dresses with lace collars. And one Christmas they all put white kid boots on their lists.

But lately no one mentioned wanting clothes like Veronica's. They preferred suede jumpers with wide zippers to Nicky's hand-stitched wools. And the rich girl in *The Castle* didn't have a single turtleneck sweater or fringed poncho.

During the day Carol had time, now and then, to think of ways to include Nicky in the activities of the weekend. *Maybe Nicky could leave Flora long enough to go skating. The weather forecast says it will be zero or below. The ice should be ready. But there'd be boys there. Would that be against Mr. Kingsbury's rules?*

She decided that someway, somehow she was going to get Betty and Nicky together. *So each will*

44

know why I think the other is so great.

She didn't see Veronica the rest of the day and had not planned to meet her after school. "I'll want to be at home when Mother leaves for the airport," Nicky had said. "She'll meet me after school. She's going to meet Daddy and go to some kind of banquet. Then he's going west. The office manager at the plant is taking her to Muncie to catch the plane."

Carol walked past the shoe store as usual on her way home. Her father was on the ladder which rolled in front of the tiers of shoe boxes. Mrs. Trent was fitting cowboy boots on a little boy. There were several empty chairs. Carol decided she wasn't needed and went on toward home.

The sun was a pale orange ball behind the gray clouds of the winter afternoon. The ropes of plastic greenery across Main Street rattled and crackled in the raw wind. Carol turned up the wide collar of her corduroy coat and hurried toward the warmth of home.

7

The delicious aroma of freshly baked bread was all around Carol when she opened the back door. Two butter crusted loaves lay on a folded white towel on the cabinet. And a pan of sugary cinnamon swirls was cooling on the table. She helped herself to one of them. There was a rule in the Retherford house that food left on the table could be eaten without asking permission.

Carol looked for a note under the Japanese teapot on the windowsill but didn't find one. *Mom's here. But where?* She listened for the sound of footsteps or of voices. The house was still except for the clicking of the copper-faced clock on the wall and the vibration of the windowpanes in the wind.

Then, as Carol started toward the stairway she heard the scraping squeak of the hinges on the back porch door. Her mother came in with the rush of cold air. "Hi, Songbird!" she said, as she set a bushel basket on the floor inside the door.

"What's in there?" Carol asked. "Besides glass jars?"

"More glass jars," Nancy Retherford said.

"For Grandfather's maple syrup?" Carol asked.

"Right!"

"Mom! It's November. The sugar water doesn't run until spring," Carol said.

"I know, I know," her mother said. "But I'm thinking of going out to Mt. Summit on Sunday. So this seemed to be a good time to gather up some jars and scrub them. By the way, did Veronica call you?"

"No," Carol said. "But what's the connection between Nicky and going to Grandfather's?"

"Well, I thought she might like to go along," Nancy said.

"That's a great idea. Really fabulous!" Carol said. "I'll ask her. Her father's going away tomorrow, I think." Just then the telephone rang.

"Carol?" Veronica said. "I thought you would *never* get home. I'm bursting with things to tell you."

"Then tell me," Carol said.

"Well, I'd rather come see you for a little while. If that's okay."

"Certainly, dash down."

"I'll have to come back before dark. Flora's still hobbling, and I wouldn't want to leave her alone too long," Veronica said. "She's getting restless and might try to do too much."

Carol hurried to the kitchen to fill her mother in on what was happening. Her sentences came out in little bursts of excitement. It all seemed so romantic. Like a story.

"What do you think Veronica's coming down to tell you?" Nancy asked.

"I don't know," Carol said. "But it's probably about Bruce — maybe about inviting him to live in the gardener's cottage."

Nancy didn't speak while hot water was filling the deep sink.

"Would you let someone stay without telling Daddy?" Carol asked.

Her mother smiled as she doused quart jars in soapy water. "That's really an unlikely question for me to ask. Our gardener's cottage is a five-foot-square shed and I'm the one who uses the tools, mainly."

"But I want to know. Would you?"

Nancy shook her head and said, "No. Not in my situation. I wouldn't have to. Your father's not a tyrant. With Joanne, things are different. But why, dear? Why are you concerned about what's right?"

"I don't know for sure," Carol said. "But I am. Maybe it's because I don't want things spoiled for Nicky. She's so *alive* and sparkly these days. Besides she wouldn't want *anyone* to get in trouble because of her. Not her mother, or Bruce, or me. I just know she wouldn't."

Veronica came to the door as Nancy patted Carol's cheek and said, "I'm *glad* I'm your mother."

The girls ran upstairs and Nicky talked as Carol changed into knit slacks and a sweatshirt.

48

"So much has happened," Veronica began, as she leaned back against the head of the bed. She told Carol that her mother had taken her shopping in Winchester. "You'll have to see!" she said. "I have two mix-and-match outfits, slacks, skirt, sweater, and all. One's turquoise, the other bittersweet. But that's not the most important thing."

Joanne had taken Nicky to a drive-in at the edge of town. They ate double cheeseburgers and chocolate milk shakes under the long striped canopy. For the first time the Kingsbury convertible was parked in the row with cars owned by workers at the glass plant and students from the college.

"At first I felt choked when I started to talk," Nicky said. "But it soon seemed easy and right. Mother made me comfortable. She understands. And she knew more than I thought. About Bruce, I mean."

"Did you ask her, or tell your idea for helping him?"

"Yes. I was a little late getting back to school," Veronica said. "But once we started talking there wasn't any stopping place."

"And?" Carol asked.

"Well, Mother said she had to think more about the plan. But before she left she made a decision. She said Bruce could stay in the cottage for the two weeks Daddy's away. Then she'll have to tell him."

"Do you think two weeks free of paying room rent will help?" Carol asked.

"Some," Veronica said. "But maybe not enough. As Mother said, though, it will be one step. And we can take the next step when we get to it."

"Do you think Bruce will agree?" Carol asked.

49

"I'm not sure. I told Mother he might not. She said she had something else in mind, but she didn't say what. She had to leave for the plant to catch her ride to the airport."

Before Nicky left, Carol asked her if she'd like to go out to Mt. Summit on Sunday. "Or can't you leave Flora?"

"Oh, I'd love to go," Veronica said. "And Flora's sister Pauline is coming over on the bus from Muncie. They'll be so busy talking and showing each other their new crochet stitches they won't even miss me."

"Well, I'll talk to you and let you know when we're leaving," Carol said.

"What will you be doing tomorrow?" Veronica asked.

"Probably helping out at the store," Carol said. "Part of the day anyway. Especially if the weather forecast is correct. We're to get more snow."

The lights on *The Castle* gateposts came on as Veronica walked out the door. Blue shadows darkened the world.

"Let me get my coat," Carol said. "I'll walk part way."

"But you'll have to come back alone," Veronica said.

"And you'll have to go on by yourself," Carol said. "But we'll both be walking toward lights."

Carol didn't expect to hear from Veronica again that night. Betty Rose came over so they could work together on Spanish. They popped corn and made cup after cup of hot spiced tea.

Several times Carol was tempted to tell Betty about Bruce's problem and Veronica's plan. But she bit her tongue and held back the words. It wouldn't be right to talk about Nicky's business.

"I wonder if the ice on the pond is thick enough for skating," Betty said as she closed her books.

"I think so," Carol said. "I saw the Andrews twins headed that way. And you know those boys! The best skaters in town. Why? What do you have in mind?"

"Oh, I thought we might gather up a bunch and go skating tomorrow night. Do you think Veronica could go? Or want to?" Betty said.

"She'd want to. But her parents are away. And Flora — you remember her — has a sprained ankle. You could *ask*."

"I will," Betty said. "See you!"

Carol's father was late getting home from work and the Retherfords had a quiet evening. Nancy stacked the shining clean jars and called her mother long-distance to tell her they'd be out on Sunday unless a blizzard came. She took down an order for groceries.

Carol played Monopoly with her father until they were both willing to quit and give up winning.

Carol went to sleep twice during a half hour television show and decided to go to bed. "I guess real life is so exciting around here now that I lose interest in TV," she said.

Then the telephone rang and Nicky told Carol the latest development. Bruce had called *The Castle* saying that Joanne Kingsbury had located him on the job, through the nursery.

"Mother must have said just exactly the right thing," Nicky said. "He's moving in the cottage tomorrow."

"What *did* she say?" Carol asked.

"That she was going away for the weekend and she'd feel better if he was near — because of Flora and me. And that the same thing would be true for two weeks, even after she came home. "Then," Nicky said, in a bashful sort of voice, "Bruce said we are to have no dates. That would be unfair."

"Can't you even *talk* to him?"

"Yes. If we see each other around. Right now Flora's sitting here fretting because she can't get down and do some cleaning. I'll do what I can."

"I'd like to help," Carol said.

"But you have to work. . . ."

"Not until noon," Carol said. "I'll be over if Mother says it's okay."

Carol started upstairs. Then she went to the kitchen. Her mother usually read a chapter from the Bible or from a book of meditations before she went to bed.

"Am I interrupting?" Carol asked.

"No. No. What's on your mind?"

"Well, I've been puzzled about something. Why wasn't I surprised when Nicky told me her mother was a nurse? And how does Mrs. Kingsbury know the color of your eyes?"

"*I* told you Joanne was a nurse. That's how I met your father. He was dating her and was in the sun-room one day when I was visiting my Aunt Rose. And she probably noticed. . . ."

"Wait a minute! My father dated Joanne Kingsbury!"

"Well, she was Joanne Ross then."

"Parents!" Carol said. "You certainly can surprise a person."

52

8

The sun came through the gray blue clouds for most of the next morning. But its light was pale, a misty silver. The radio newscasts kept predicting more snow by nightfall or by early morning.

Nancy Retherford gave Carol permission to help Veronica. "But save enough time and energy to clean your own room. I'm helping at the store all day."

"Should I come on down or call first to see if you need help?"

"Call first," Nancy said. "But you'd better come home about eleven-thirty. That'll give you time to shower and change in case we need a hand."

"I will," Carol said. "We should have the place cleaned before then. It's not that big, or that dirty."

Veronica was ready to go to the cottage when Carol reached *The Castle*. She had a pail filled with sponges, soft cloths, soap powder, and floor wax.

"We'll have to come back . . . two or three times . . . for the mops and brooms," Veronica said. "And Flora had me dig out some linen drapes, blankets, and throw rugs from the attic. They'll provide the finishing touches."

As the girls crossed the brick terrace outside the back door someone rapped on the kitchen window. Flora, dressed in heavy coat sweater and long wool scarf, motioned for them to wait.

When she came out the door, Nicky said, "Flora! What are you doing?"

"What do you think?" Flora said. "I'm going with you."

"But you. . . ."

"Don't say I shouldn't. I know that. But for the first time in a mighty long time this place is coming to life. And I'm not aiming to sit on the sidelines. You girls run on. I'll catch up . . . by and by."

Veronica smiled. "What can I say? But please be careful. There *are* icy places."

The next two hours seemed to be swallowed in one big gulp of activity. Carol swept, Veronica mopped, and Flora dusted.

"Have you ever mopped floors before?" Carol asked.

"Sure," Veronica said. "Down here when Alexandra and I played house."

The girls rolled a folding bed out of the room which was not to be used and put it in the walled-in corner. Flora showed them how to hook drapes on

54

Nicky and Carol moved a white wicker couch with a
yellow, linen-covered pad under the pair of windows.

traverse rods and Carol already knew how to folk box corners on sheets.

"It's looking better all the time," Veronica said. "The kitchen's fine. But this room's sort of bare. With just the bed and library table and bookshelves."

"It needs easy chairs or a couch," Flora said. "Are you sure you looked under all the old blankets in the storeroom? It seems we sent some stuff down here when your mother redid the sun-room."

Nicky and Carol bumped into each other in their rush to make new discoveries. They soon had a white wicker couch with a yellow linen covered pad under the pair of windows. The matching chair and round lamp table made the room look livable and inviting.

"It needs two things," Flora said as she sat down on the couch and put her foot on the small table. "A lamp. And the picnic basket of victuals. It's on the kitchen table."

"Victuals?" Nicky said.

"Food," Carol said. "Haven't you ever heard the word victuals?"

"No, I don't think so," Veronica said.

"My grandmother uses it. Is it a country word, Flora?" Carol asked.

"I don't think so," Flora said. "This is as near country as I know. I can't think why you never heard me use it. Maybe I don't. Maybe it's not fitting or proper in the big house. Anyways you girls scoot. It's getting late."

They came back with two lamps, an old bridge light, and one with a pottery base for the study table.

The basket of food was unpacked and stored in the small refrigerator and cabinet above the sink. Flora

56

had gathered bread, cold cuts, molasses cookies, apples, bananas, cereal, and milk. "This was sweet of you," Nicky said.

"Well, the way things have been, that many leftovers go to waste every week. So I figured I'd bring this much down here before it got to be leftover. Give that young man a bit of a start."

"When do you think Bruce will come?" Carol asked as they trudged back to *The Castle*. They were tired, but pleased about the results of their morning's work.

"When he gets off work and gets back to town," Veronica said. "He'll use a nursery truck to move his clothes and books. You know, Carol, you asked if two weeks of free rent would help. Actually he will have five. Christmas vacation will come right after the end of the term. If he can't stay here he can go home or rent a room. Cheaper than the dorm."

"That should give him time to save up a nest egg," Flora said.

Carol helped carry the cleaning materials into the house, then she hurried down the driveway. Halfway along she remembered, *I didn't say anything about going skating. I wonder if Betty will call and if Nicky will go.*

After Carol called the shoe store she took time to rest for half an hour. "We can get by until two," Nancy Retherford said. "Mrs. Trent's helping out for a couple of hours."

Scrambled eggs, salad, and fruit Jello were Carol's quick lunch. Then she cleaned her room before dressing to go downtown.

She barely had time to look up for three hours. Purses, shoes, boots, and hosiery were being thrust at her for packaging. The rush let up a little before five. Carol was filing the duplicate sales slips when she heard a child's voice.

She looked up to see a tall young man who was holding a little boy. Both had bronze red hair and clear blue eyes. The child kept leaning over trying to see his new red leather boots. "See!" he said. "Pretty, pretty!"

"Yes, Cowboy! They're pretty. But straighten up! You're breaking your dad's arms," the man said.

"Let me take him," a soft voice said. "So you can reach your billfold."

Carol glanced at the tall slender girl with smoky black hair. She looked vaguely familiar. *Who is she?*

The young mother smiled at Carol, then took the little boy over to touch a papier-maché Pilgrim. After the boy's boots were sacked and change made the child ran to his father. His steps were awkward in the large stiff boots.

The couple started up the aisle. Then the girl came back. "I just have to tell you how grateful I am for your kindness and friendliness toward my sister."

"Oh!" Carol said. "You're Alexandra! I thought I should know you. But I couldn't. . . ."

"That's not surprising," Alexandra Kingsbury Weaver said. "You didn't start to high school until I was out. And we didn't get around much. But perhaps Veronica will. Thanks to you. I do hope so.

"You don't owe me any thanks. It's easy to be nice to Nicky. I like her."

Alexandra called her husband back and introduced him proudly. Who could help but see how happy they were? Mr. Arthur I. Kingsbury, Jr., must be wearing a blindfold. *But he doesn't need one. He doesn't go to see Alexandra.*

Carol and her mother left the store at the same time. They went to the supermarket. Nancy needed coconut to make her German chocolate cake. "Papa would be a little disappointed if I went home without one," she said.

The grocery store was crowded. A few flakes of snow began sifting through the air as darkness came. "Everyone's rushing for supplies," Nancy said.

"I wonder about Flora and Veronica," she said. "If they need anything."

"I never thought of that," Carol said. "How *do* they get food. Does anyone in town deliver?"

"I don't really know," Nancy said. "But why don't you call? There's a telephone booth at the back. Here's a dime."

Veronica answered and was relieved when she heard the reason for the call. "Oh, Carol, we do. Somehow Mother forgot to order bread. And with Flora's sister coming, could you get some? I'll run down and pick it up when you get home."

"Will do!" Carol said. "Anything else?"

There was a pause while Nicky talked to Flora. She was laughing when she turned to say, "It sounds silly, but Flora's hungry for Cracker Jack. She wants to know if they still make them."

"They sure do! In checkerboard boxes," Carol said. "With prizes."

"Then bring us four boxes, Flora says. If it isn't too much trouble."

"Did Bruce move in?" Carol asked.

"Yes. About two hours ago. He stopped by for the

key. Then he came back to tell us how great everything looked and to thank us. We told him you helped."

"He didn't stay long?" Carol said.

"No. Just a few minutes, while Flora brought her old radio for him to use."

Carol was about ready to hang up when Veronica said, "Betty called about going skating."

"Oh, are you?" Carol asked.

"Yes. Bruce and Flora arranged a signal. She's to turn on the light in front of the greenhouse if she needs anything. He can see it."

"He's not going?" Carol asked.

"No. I mentioned it. But he said that would be taking unfair advantage."

9

Nancy Retherford made a pot of creamy potato soup for dinner. It simmered while she mixed her cake. "I don't know how long your father will be at the store," she said. "The soup will keep . . . and be- sides, it's easy. This has been a long day."

"I know," Carol said. "For me, too. Now that I'm in where it's warm I'd rather not go to the pond . . . out into the cold."

"Do you have to go?" Nancy asked.

"Well, I guess not really. But Betty would be hurt. And I *did* promise. I'd better use steel wool on my ice skates. They're probably rusty."

As she opened the back door she nearly collided with a young man in a Windbreaker and high boots.

"Jeff!" Carol said. "You're home!"

"Evidently," Jeff Stafford said.

"Come on in," Nancy said. "Did you smell my cake sampler?"

"Not until I got to the door," Jeff said. "But my timing is sure great."

"Why are you home?" Carol asked. "Get expelled or something?"

"You know better than that. Squares like yours truly never get kicked out."

He sat down astraddle a kitchen chair and took off his knit cap.

"Well, you know what I say about this label *square*," Nancy said.

"I know . . . some things in this world are supposed to be square and you're one. Quote, unquote. So am I," Jeff said.

"But you didn't say . . . why are you home?"

"A fellow down the hall has an aunt who lives here. He has a car and was driving up. So I came. Any objections?"

Carol smiled. "No objections. Some kids are going skating later."

"I know. I ran into Betty Rose as I came down the alley. I included myself in."

"Great. We're meeting here at seven."

"Then I'd better go," Jeff said. "Mom wants me to pick up some stuff at the store. See you. Thanks for the handout, Mrs. R."

After Jeff left Nancy smiled at Carol. "I thought you were too tired to want to go skating. Do I detect a new enthusiasm now?"

"Well," Carol said. "You know how it is."

Betty had gathered up nine people before the group met at Carol's. Not couples, just people. There were five girls and four boys and the addition and Veronica made the balance more lopsided. "I had competition — a basketball game over at the college," Betty said. "I was lucky to snatch this many men."

"That's the way she did it. By calling us *men*," Dane Andrews said. "I just caught on!"

"Plus one other thing," his twin Dave added. "Flattering us about our skating."

Betty's creamy cheeks looked flushed even in the mellow lamplight. What Dave Andrews said was important to her. She was tuned his way.

"Well, that's not how she got me to go along," Jeff said. "Not by bragging on my skating! She knows that a leaf frozen into the ice can send me into a tailspin."

The group left the house and Betty led them across the street. "Why is she going this way?" Jeff asked.

"To pick up Veronica," Carol said.

"You mean the Princess?" Jeff said. "Since when did she decide to associate with the plebeians?"

"Since the day she stopped me in the hall and I realized how lonely she is," Carol said. She told them as much as she had time to say, and all that she cared to reveal. "Her parents are away and that's why she's coming along. She couldn't if her father were here."

"He's afraid she'll elope like Sandy?" Jeff said.

"Sandy? I never heard anyone call Alexandra that."

"Well, I don't," Jeff said. "But Corby does."

"You know him?" Carol asked.

"Sure, my dad and I built his second station last summer. He's a great guy."

By this time Betty was lifting the brass knocker on the heavy double doors. Veronica asked everyone in, but they said the lights were to be on at the pond only until nine.

"Then when you come back," Nicky said. "Flora showed me how to make pigs in blankets. They're ready to pop into the oven."

"The Princess cooks," Jeff whispered to Carol.

"Don't let her hear you," Carol said. "She doesn't want to be different.

Carol glanced toward the gardener's cottage, but the evergreen trees hid it from her view. No light could be seen from the front. She wished Bruce could go with them. *But as Mom would say, I'm rushing things. Trying to eat tomorrow's dinner today.*

The next hour and a half was pure and exhilarating pleasure. Two of the eleven known as the Randolph Avenue gang were in college, and all of them had developed new patterns of friendship. And Veronica's presence in the group was a new factor. But in the weightless motion of skating on the milky ice the years and the differences disappeared, floated away in the frost-flecked air.

"It's like a white and crystal fairyland," Veronica said as she and Carol warmed their hands at a charcoal burner on the bank.

The bushes along the edge were whiskered in white. And the snow was sprinkled with dancing, sparkling pinpoints.

Everyone's toes were a little numb as they headed back up the street to *The Castle*. Veronica sent all her guests but Carol and Betty to the library. "There's a fire," she said. "Flora and I have kept it

64

going all night and all day. Neither of us is good at kindling a new fire."

The three girls carried trays of sizzling hot dogs wrapped in crusty, flaky dough to the skaters who washed the food down with quarts of foamy hot chocolate.

Nicky turned the hi-fi low. Music, talk, and laughter filled the paneled room and spilled out over the rest of the big house.

Betty Rose took hold of Carol's wrist after they'd carried trays of empty plates and cups to the kitchen. "I want to thank you for something. For opening my eyes so I could see Nicky clearly. Isn't she . . . super!"

"Yes," Carol said. "And you've been great to ask her tonight."

Before the skaters left *The Castle,* Carol told Veronica, "We'll leave for Grandmother's right after church. About 11:45. We'll pick you up."

Veronica smiled. "I'll be ready. Then she suddenly looked wistful.

"Something wrong?"

"Oh, I was wishing I could go to church with you. I never have."

"Never gone to church!" Carol said.

"Not here in town," Nicky said. "And no place very often."

"You could go," Carol said. "We'd be happy to have you."

"I know," Nicky said. "But I'd better not. Someone at the plant might see me and mention it to Daddy. He'd be furious. And I'd probably be dragged on business trips forever after."

Jeff went along home with Carol and stayed at the Retherfords for over an hour.

"When are you going back?" Carol asked him.

"About one tomorrow," he said. "It takes a good four hours to get to Evansville. And Sam and I have to study for an eight o'clock exam. Will you be around in the morning?"

"Well . . . at church. Then we're going on to Mt. Summit afterward. Nicky's going with us."

"She surprised me tonight," Jeff said. "I've always thought of her as stiff and aloof. A little like a big doll. A very well-dressed doll."

"Yes. You're right," Carol said. "She did seem sort of unreal. But we were wrong."

After Jeff had left, Carol wondered how Mr. A. J. Kingsbury, Jr., would have acted if he'd have come home unexpectedly. *Would he have rushed us all out of the house with a never-darken-my-door kind of remark?*

We'd have probably done our own rushing, Carol thought. *Why does even the thought of that man scare us?*

But that's not the right kind of thinking, Carol told herself as she turned out the lights in her room and crawled into bed. She turned over and looked out the window at the familiar sight of the twin globes on *The Castle* gateposts.

Snatches of the evening flitted in and out of her thoughts. It was as if a movie projector was out of control running forward, backward, and skipping around.

She could see one lighted window in the second story of the Kingsbury house. *That's Veronica's room.*

66

I know now. Somehow the big white brick structure didn't seem so isolated as before. Not so set apart.

Just before Carol floated into sleep, she thought of what Nicky had said about going to church. Why would Nicky's father object? How could anything be wrong with going to church?"

10

As soon as Carol opened her eyes she knew it was Sunday. She didn't have to climb out of the deep feather bed of sleep and wonder where she was. Her nose told her.

The Retherfords always had hot biscuits and creamed chipped beef for breakfast on Sunday. It was a custom. Now as Carol stretched and yawned, the fragrance of buttery biscuits told her it was time to get up.

She looked out of the window. The lights on *The Castle* gateposts were still on. For the first time Carol realized that the globes were not turned on automatically. They weren't like the barnyard light on her grandfather's farm. Someone in the big house flicked

68

a switch or pushed a button every night and morning. *Flora and Nicky are probably sleeping late. After last night's excitement,* Carol thought. She wore a striped shift downstairs. It was her candy cane dress, as her little cousin called it. The Retherfords began their day as soon as they rose. They didn't postpone activity by wearing nightclothes while they worked.

Carol's father was reading the magazine section of the Sunday paper. This was another part of the special quality of Sunday. Mr. Retherford didn't have to hurry to get to the store.

"Good morning, Songbird," he said. No one else in the world except her parents linked the name Carol to singing and birds. And it wouldn't have seemed right for others to do so. This was their private nickname. Secretly Carol thought they were a little inaccurate because her voice wasn't that good. But she did love to sing, as her mother put it, for her own use.

"Hi, Daddy," Carol said. "It's sort of gloomy outside, isn't it? Do you think it's going to snow more?"

He smiled at her over the top of the brightly colored pages. "Afraid you won't get to go to Mt. Summit?"

"Maybe," she admitted.

"Well, it's not likely it'll keep us from going or coming back," her father answered. "But as for tomorrow, who knows?"

Carol started toward the kitchen when she heard the squeak of a door.

"Say!" Mr. Retherford said. "Here's an article about Henry County! About the minister who spearheads the drive to collect clothing and food for the Navahos."

69

Nancy came to the doorway. "And toys," she said. "I have two boxes of things I've been gathering up. Mother has her gifts ready also. We plan to take them into the fire station on Trojan Lane today sometime."

"Well, it looks as if we've got a full day ahead. I'd better get moving," Carol's father said.

After breakfast Carol helped stow boxes and baskets in the back of the station wagon. Then she dressed for church and packed knit slacks, a pullover sweater, and her corduroy coat for walking around the farm.

The Retherfords arrived at the red brick church as the last bell was ringing. This place and the feeling it gave Carol was another part of the meaning of Sunday. Light came through the stained glass of the arched windows, making a lovely pattern on all it touched. The harmony of the hymns was like kind words and gentle touches. *Mother's right*, Carol thought, *when she says that Sunday is both a blessing and a benediction to the week.*

Veronica was waiting at the bowed window when the station wagon came up the drive. She hurried out wearing a soft plush coat of mint green and matching knit slacks. *That's too good*, Carol thought, *for prowling around the sugar camp. But maybe Nicky doesn't have any old clothes.*

On the way out State Road 3 Veronica said, "I didn't know what to wear, but finally decided on this coat. It's so warm and I'm about to outgrow it. Look. The sleeves come up to here."

The lovely girl who'd seemed like a princess in a castle for so long entered into the activity of the day

70

with enthusiasm and she blended with the warmth of
a loving family. She ate two helping of Grandmother's
baked dumplings and said they looked like crusty pil-
lows.

After the noon meal which was still called dinner
in the country, Nancy asked, "Do you girls want to go
into town with us?"

Carol looked at Nicky, "Do we?"

"You decide."

"I'd rather stay here," Carol said. "We don't have
much time. Daddy has to get back by six for a Men's
Fellowship meeting at the church."

"Let's stay then," Veronica said.

Later as the girls bundled themselves in their warm
coats and added wool scarves, Nicky said. I'm glad
you have to be home by six. I was a little worried
that we might be late."

"On account of Flora?"

"No, not that. Her sister's staying until eight. Some
neighbor is picking her up then. But I'm not sure
when Mother and maybe even Daddy will get back
from Chicago.

A shadow seemed to have fallen on Veronica's
bright mood. Carol knew why. *She's afraid everything will be spoiled. That her father won't want her
to be friends with me. Or that he'll find out that Bruce
is in the gardener's cottage.*

Carol couldn't imagine how anyone could not know
what was going on in his own home, not even a place
as large as *The Castle. Her* father would know. He was
a walker and an observer. He saw every broken twig
on the pair of flowering plum trees and not one
shingle could be ruffled by the wind without Tom

Retherford knowing about it and repairing the damage.

Carol had spoken to Nicky about this while they cleaned the cottage. "How can your father *not* see that someone's down here?"

"That's easy," Nicky said. "He can tell you where every single box and bottle is at the Kingsbury Industries. But at home he's apart. He eats, sleeps, and rest of the time he withdraws, goes into his upstairs study, and works on books, or makes long-distance business calls. Oh, I think he reads a little . . . sometimes."

Now as the girls crossed the backyard, Carol felt like touching Nicky. Compassion filled her thoughts. She wanted to erase the shadow.

"Let's hurry to the Sugar House," she said. The frozen grass crackled under their boots and soft wet snow began to hit their cheeks before they reached the long wooden shed.

"Draw a deep breath and hold it as you go in the door," Carol said. "Now inhale. What do you smell?"

"Maple!" Nicky said. "It's all mapley."

"I know," Carol said. "You should be here in the spring when they're boiling sugar water. Flavored steam rolls up from that long tank day and night. It soaks into the rafters and the walls. That's what you smell now. But when the sap begins to run . . . well, you'll have to come out with us then to know how delicious it is."

"I hope I can," Veronica said.

The girls went into the storage room and saw the metal spouts which were driven into trees, and the plastic bags which caught the sugar water. "I saw

72

a picture of a maple syrup operation," Nicky said. "Pails were hanging on the sides of trees."

"Granddad used to do that too. And he has a few left. But plastic bags are better. They keep the dirt out," Carol said.

The girls walked into the nearest grove and saw a few of the three thousand tall, straight trees which were tapped every year. By this time their toes were tingling, almost numb from the cold.

They went back to the house, kicked off their shoes, and warmed their feet on the hot air register in the floor. Carol's grandfather teased them into playing a game of double nine dominoes. Her father brought in wedges of chocolate cake and later the girls made hot tea for everyone.

"It's sure taking the womenfolk a long time to deliver their donations," Carol's grandfather said. "New Castle's not that far away."

"You really didn't expect them to come right back," his son-in-law said. "Not with all the relatives they have around town."

"No. To tell the truth I didn't. But if I let on I'd expected them to be late, I'd be depriving myself of grumbling material."

Nancy and her mother returned before five. The swapping, as Nancy's father called it, began. The baskets which came out with glass jars, German chocolate cake, and scraps for quilts were repacked with eggs, frozen meat, and as always, a quart of maple syrup.

"I tell you, Tom," Nancy's father said, "there's no doubt in my mind that you'd get an extra year's use out of your automobile if you could break these women of their bartering. No ordinary springs or shock absorbers can take the strain."

On the way home, Veronica said, "It's been such fun. I've never felt so free and warm and good in my life."

"Didn't Grandfather's teasing bother you?" Carol asked.

"Well . . . maybe a little at first. But then I saw that none of you seemed upset. And I saw the twinkle in his eyes."

As the pulled up to the Kingsbury drive, Veronica drew a breath of relief. "They're not home," she whispered.

"How can you tell from here?" Carol asked.

"There's no light in my father's study."

"I just happened to think," Carol said. "I thought your father was flying on to California?"

"He planned to," Nicky said. "But if the weather's bad, he might come home first."

Before Nicky climbed out, Nancy handed her a package. "Here, my mother sent this. It's a jar of syrup."

"Oh, how sweet," Nicky said. "I'll see if Flora will show me how to make hot cakes for dinner. If we're alone. Thank you so much . . . for everything. See you tomorrow, Carol."

11

The Retherfords had only been home a few minutes when Carol saw the sweep of car lights on the stone gatepost across the street. She looked out in time to see a taxi going around the curve in the drive. It was too dark to be sure how many people were with the driver, one or two.

She knew that Veronica hoped that her father would go on to California. She didn't say that she and her mother would be happier if he were away. But there was no need. A flat tone came in Nicky's voice when she spoke of any phase of Arthur J. Kingsbury's attitudes or actions.

For two weeks . . . if he's gone . . . they'll feel free, Carol thought as she opened her books. There hadn't been much time for homework. *I wonder if they'll have Alexandra and the Little Weaver up. Or would she even want to come, knowing how her father feels?*

Again the little whispers of doubt came to Carol. How much of what was going on in the Kingsbury family was right? And what was wrong? *The Bible tells us to honor our parents. Is helping Bruce and being friends with me, dishonorable?*

Carol shook her head as if to clear it of the puzzling cobwebby thoughts. She needed a clear mind to translate the page and a half of Spanish.

Silence seemed to awaken her the next morning. At least that was what she was aware of when she began to be conscious of the world around her. Usually cars streamed by on the way to the glass plant. Randolph Street was the widest access to Winchester from the farms and towns to the east.

Carol raised up and leaned on one elbow. *The world seems muffled.* That could only mean one thing. Snow. She hurried to the window. A fluffy white blanket had been spread during the night. The rose bushes were tufted bumps in the covering. The spikes of the iron fence across the street wore snowy caps.

And snow was still falling in a flaked curtain. Carol realized why she didn't hear the morning traffic. It was running on a fluffy cushion. The tracks of one car were nearly filled before the next one came along.

She wondered if there'd be school. Sometimes the buses from outlying townships were ordered to stay off the roads if hazardous driving conditions were predicted.

But I might as well get ready. It'd take a blow-

ing blizzard before us town kids would be told to stay at home.

Carol's father was leaving to go to the store when she reached the kitchen. "Why so early, Daddy?" she asked.

"I'll have to do some shoveling to get out of the garage," he answered. "And I think I'll put the tire chains on. From what the weatherman said, I may need them to get back home."

"Why? Is it going to get worse?" Carol asked.

"Yes," Nancy Retherford said. "The snow's to keep coming until evening. And strong winds are forecast for the early afternoon. You know what that means."

"Drifts," Carol said. "With this much snow they could be really high."

"I know," Nancy said. "I'm glad I took it on myself to buy extra groceries for Mother. I hate to think of them being snowbound."

Carol was pulling on her angora mittens when the doorbell rang. Her mother hurried to answer it, then Nicky's voice was saying, "Would Carol want to ride with us?"

"I'm sure she would," Nancy said. "Your mother's brave to get out on a morning like this."

"It's a case of necessity," Nicky said. "The weather's so bad she thinks we'd better lay in supplies. And she wants me to ask about the best place to buy meat. Daddy always insists we have things brought over from Muncie. That we not play favorites by buying things at any store in town."

"I see," Nancy said. "Well, I think the meat market on the east side of the courthouse square is the best."

After Carol was downstairs she heard Nicky say,

"Lately it's like we're discovering Winchester and I've lived here all my life."

Joanne Kingsbury drove slowly and cautiously, avoiding quick turns, and coasting to a stop instead of using the brakes. "I don't take many chances," she said. "Do you girls want me to pick you up at 3:15?"

"Why don't we walk?" Nicky said. "When you get back you may want to stay by the fire."

"Besides that," Carol said, "We may not stay all day. Only three buses made it down our street and the principal may decide it will be safer to let them go home before the wind rises."

The girls had only a few minutes to talk before they went to class. "Have you seen Bruce?" Carol asked.

"No," Nicky said. "He's sticking to the agreement. Mother ran down and talked to him for half an hour last night. That's another reason she's going shopping this morning . . . to get paint."

"Paint?" Carol asked.

"For the cottage," Nicky said. "There's the bell. I'll tell you about it later."

As Carol halfway expected, school was dismissed after the students ate lunch. Mr. Griffin, the principal, made the announcement over the address system. His voice echoed in all the halls and classrooms. "The roads are filling in and the wind is rising. The three township buses will leave immediately. All in-city students may stay for lunch if they choose to do so."

Betty Rose, Veronica, and Carol walked home together. The northeast wind wasn't bitterly cold but

78

it plastered wet snow on their clothes and faces.

"Do you think we'll have school tomorrow?" Betty Rose asked as they came to her corner.

"I doubt it," Carol said. "Mr. Griffin told us to listen to the Early Bell news over the radio."

"Then we'll have to plan something, a winter sport type of fun."

"Well! This is certainly the right kind of weather," Nicky said

"I'll be calling you," Betty said as she plowed through the ridged drift across the sidewalk.

Veronica went in when they came to the Retherford home. She called her mother and said she'd be home a little later.

Carol's mother was not at home. She'd left a note saying she'd gone up the alley to see if Mrs. Prentiss, a neighbor, needed anything.

The girls sat at the kitchen table and talked. Nicky said that her mother was buying paint for Bruce to use on the cottage. He'd insisted on working out his rent.

"So your mother thought of this way to make him feel better about staying," Carol said.

"That's what I thought . . . at first," Nicky said. "But my mother has an idea in her mind. For the future."

She told Carol that Joanne Kingsbury worked in the Children's Ward of the Fort Wayne Hospital. She'd seen children dismissed and sent to homes where there was not enough loving care for healing to continue. Often they had relapses and were brought back for longer periods.

"Mother wants to make the cottage into a kind of

convalescent home," Veronica said. "She thinks she could take as many as six at a time. She'd work some of the time and hopes to find a way to pay a full-time practical nurse."

"What do you think?" Carol asked.

"I wonder what Father will say," Veronica said. "You know, Carol, for the first time, in such a long time, I don't think he will say no. Or even try to change Mother's mind."

"Why? What makes you feel this way?" Carol asked.

"Oh, I don't know for sure," Veronica said. "It's something in Mother's voice . . . in the way she looked when she talked about her plans. There was a kind of light. A determination. Like she couldn't be blocked."

As Nicky was leaving, her mother called. After a few minutes, Veronica turned to Carol. "Guess what! We're having company! Alexandra's coming to eat with us. Corby too . . . and the baby. Mother wants you to come."

Carol started to accept the invitation. Then she smiled and shook her head. "Not this time, Nicky. This is special. A family time. You can ask me later."

"You're sweet," Veronica said. "I'll talk to you to-morrow . . . or sooner."

At first Carol felt lost, having an extra afternoon and perhaps longer without homework or plans. She felt unanchored until Mrs. Trent called.

"Carol? I wonder, would you like to help me out this afternoon For a couple of hours?"

"Yes, certainly. Doing what? And how'd you know I was home?" Carol asked.

"Oh, that's not a mystery," Mrs. Trent said. "The boys next door, and a half a dozen friends, are building a snow fort. And I've seen at least three snowball fights . . . one of which needed a referee. Meaning me."

Mrs. Trent told Carol that she was working on her personal Christmas project of making velvet and bead Christmas tree decorations for the nursing and convalescent homes for miles around.

"I'd love to help," Carol said. "They're so beautiful. But I thought you said you had everyone supplied."

"I know," Mrs. Trent said, "so I thought. But I've learned that those who are in bed rarely see the trees. So I'm making some ornaments to hang on their beds or lamps . . . or for them to hold in their hands, to touch."

"I'll be there," Carol said.

12

Carol decided she'd better not wait until her mother came home to get her permission to go to the Trents. If Mrs. Prentiss needed groceries or anything, Nancy would see that the need was filled.

"I'll leave a note. She can call me at Mrs. Trent's if I'm needed."

As Carol crossed over to Madison Street she saw Sally Blane coming from the direction of Betty Rose's home. Sally was walking with her head down, swinging her fringed and beaded purse in vicious little jerks. *Oh! Oh! She's angry. Why, this time?*

If there'd been a way to avoid Sally, Carol would have taken it. She wasn't exactly proud of this feeling. The two girls had grown up together and been in the same class a lot of the time. But they'd never been friends, not really. It was like Betty had once said. "Sally has so much. Beautiful clothes . . . almost as nice as Veronica's, more spending money than any of us, and a lot of freedom. So, why is she so miserable and hateful to everyone?"

Within two houses of the Trents, Sally looked up. She started to smile, then her mouth curled up at one corner in a kind of sneer. Sometimes Carol wished Sally would look in a mirror and see how her expressions altered her appearance. *She's really lovely when her thoughts and words aren't mean.* The beauty of her red-gold hair and the gray green eyes was dimmed by her attitudes. *Is it that way with everyone?*

"Well, hello, Carrie," Sally said. "Out slumming? All by yourself? Where's your sidekick? Lady Bountiful?"

"If you mean Veronica . . . she's at home." Then she tried to change the subject by asking, "What are you going to do with the free afternoon?"

For a second Sally looked lonely . . . sort of lost. Then she said, "Oh, I'm on my way to the Nook. To meet this really groovy boy. No one you'd know."

Carol almost bit her tongue in the effort to keep from saying what she was thinking. The Nook was a college kids' hangout. In a cellar, dark and shadowy, someone had said. Carol had never wanted to go and if she had there'd be no chance her parents would approve.

All she could think of to say was, "I didn't know you went over there."

"Why not?" Sally said. "We're not babies clinging

to our mothers' skirts . . . or are you?"

As the tall girl in the high boots flipped down the
street, Carol wondered as she had many times before, *Why do some kids think it's so terrible to care
what parents say, or have them care what you do?*
Mrs. Trent met Carol at the door. She had her
wicker sewing basket under one arm. "Isn't this terrible?" she said. "Asking a pretty young girl to help
me on this holiday from school."

"I'm glad you called," Carol said. "Mother's taking care of Mrs. Prentiss and I didn't have any homework. And I think what you're doing is so great. I
want to help."

"Well, I know that," Julia Trent said, "or I would
not have called." Then she squinted her blue eyes.
"Or maybe I would have. Sooner or later."

"You have something on your mind. Something
besides velvet and pearls," Carol said.

"Yes, I confess," Mrs. Trent said. "But let's get
started at our stitching. Then we can chatter."

She set up a folding table and took materials from
a cardboard carton. Some ornaments were to be
diamond shaped, others round. Stacks of red, green,
purple, gold, and silver velvet were in two shapes —
orange-slice crescents for the round ball, triangles for
the diamonds. Mrs. Trent seamed the sections to cover
Styrofoam forms and Carol beaded the seams with
pearls, rhinestones, and sequins.

Mrs. Trent said, "I've had a good year . . . at
rummage sales, I mean. A lot of Winchester people
discarded costume jewelry."

"So that's where you get all these beads?" Carol
said.

"That's where. And by begging my friends and family," Mrs. Trent said.

As they worked, the wind became stronger. Sometimes the whirling clouds of snow kept them from seeing the houses on the opposite side of Madison Street. The oil furnace clicked off and on.

"It's going to be bad out tonight," Mrs. Trent said. "The state police post at Pendleton is issuing warnings for people to staff off the roads, especially those running north and south."

Carol thought of her grandparents and was glad they'd taken extra supplies. But as Nancy Retherford said, "Granddad would probably rather we hadn't. Blocked roads and a storm are sort of a challenge to him. He likes to climb on his big red tractor and prove he can get where others can't."

Mrs. Trent went to the kitchen and brought back a plate of doughnuts and blue willowware mugs of hot tea.

"You made these for me?" Carol asked.

"I did," Mrs. Trent said. "You're my very best doughnut customer. We may get some sugar on our sewing. But a little sweetness never hurt anyone."

Carol was sewing small gold and white daisies from an old bracelet onto the crescent shaped red velvet ball. Mrs. Trent was threading her needle when she began to tell what was on her mind. The minister had called a meeting of the various church committees. "He was concerned that we are not giving our members enough service opportunities," Mrs. Trent said.

She told Carol that the final opinion was that many people were willing to serve if they were given direction and felt that the activity had real purpose. The

85

people at the meeting agreed to survey the feelings of various groups. "And I'm to talk to young people," Mrs. Trent said. "How about that! Me! A person two generation gaps from you."

"Now Mrs. T., you know better than that," Carol said. "We've talked about this before. The generations . . . how did you put it . . . always *lap*. But we can communicate by caring and understanding."

"I believe you're right," Julia Trent said. "Like on the business of freedom. Sometimes I think young people are really saying, 'Care about me,' when they get so worked up about being free."

Right away Carol thought of Sally Blane. Was she wanting her career-minded mother to care where she went? *But I have more important things to say to Mrs. Trent today.*

"Do you think people in your church group would like some project?" Mrs. Trent asked.

"Yes, I do," Carol said. "Oh, we belong to enough stuff. At school especially. But . . . well, sometimes I wonder why I go to meetings like Camera Club."

"I suppose the big problem is to find a need you'd want to fill. Like working with the migrant children in summer," Mrs. Trent said. "That was mentioned. And being candy stripers at the hospital. Or visiting nursing homes."

All at once things went together in Carol's mind. "Oh, Mrs. T.," she said. "I may know something!" She hurried on, telling what was happening in the Kingsbury home. The sentences all ran together in a kind of eager, bubbling flow, like the white foamed water ran over the rock in Cabin Creek.

She ended with Joanne Kingsbury's plan to turn

86

the gardener's cottage into a convalescent home. "It seems to me that there'd be a lot of things we could do to help," Carol said.

"Without a doubt," Mrs. Trent said.

"We could play games, take them for walks, feed them, and all sorts of things," Carol said.

"And even tutor those who need it," Mrs. Trent added. "This is such a fine thing for Mrs. Kingsbury, to want to do. But I'm not too surprised that she'd have such feelings."

"You're not? Do you know her?"

"Not really," Mrs. Trent said. "But I did know her family. She came from Spiceland over in Henry County — my home community. Her mother and Aunt Martha were always busy helping other people."

Carol knew it was time to talk to Mrs. Trent about whether it was right for her to want Bruce and Nicky to be able to see each other, or if it was right that he was staying in the cottage, or even that she and Nicky were friends.

Carol put the fifth velvet ornament in the nest of crumpled white tissue paper. And she said, "Do you know something? It's like a thread has been running through this whole conversation . . . leading to an opening."

"So I'm not the only one with something on her mind," Mrs. Trent said.

"No," Carol said. "For days I've wondered what you'd think. Is it wrong for Nicky and her mother to want to go against Mr. Kingsbury? Or for me to think they're doing the right thing?"

Mrs. Trent picked up the scissors and clipped a strand of silver thread.

"I can't see that you've done anything wrong," she said. "Is kindness and friendliness ever wrong? And Veronica's never really met Bruce at your house has she?"

"No. It didn't work out that way. But I thought of offering." Carol said.

"You know," Mrs. Trent said, "we can't do anyone's thinking for them or obey God for them anymore than one sunray can shine for another."

Carol drew a deep breath of relief. It was as if light suddenly shone through a cloud of doubt. "One more thing," she said. "Do you think Nicky and her mother are doing wrong?"

"Well, I'm not a judge. But from what I know," Mrs. Trent said, "it seems to me that wrongs are being corrected, not committed. Bitterness and domination shouldn't rule in any house . . . not even in *The Castle!*"

13

The wind was blowing so hard that Carol wished she could walk backward while she was going home. *But I'd better watch where I'm stepping or I'll lose a boot in a drift.*

She kept her head down and didn't open her mouth. The rush of air would take her breath. She didn't see a single automobile until she turned up her own street. A white truck, a wrecker, was going toward the Kingsbury grounds. As it came even with Carol, the driver blew the horn and she could see a hand waving behind the steamy glass.

She knew that Corby Weaver had come to eat with his family and take them home. He probably thought the wrecker was needed to get through the snow.

The minute she opened the door Carol knew her mother has invited someone over either for dinner or afterward. The blended aroma of popcorn and maple syrup filled the room. *Mom's making her maple Cracker Jack.*

But who would be coming on a night like this? It had to be someone who lived near.

Her mother wasn't in the kitchen, but two rectangular pans of nut sprinkled popcorn were on the cabinet. The house was warm in spite of the whirling whistling wind. Home always seemed a sheltering place to Carol. But on winter nights like this she appreciated it more and had the feeling she was pulling its protection around her as if it were a warm blanket.

She walked into the living room and heard her mother coming downstairs. "Well, I wondered where you were! *And* who's coming."

"How do you know anyone's coming?" Nancy asked. "Is there any law that says I'm prohibited from making *us* some Cracker Jack?"

"No. But you never do for us alone," Carol said. "Besides, there are other signs."

"Like what?" Nancy asked.

"Like the pink lunch cloth with the fringe . . . and six of your big crystal cups out on the cabinet. So, tell!"

Nancy smiled and sat down on the couch. She patted the cushion beside her. "Sit, and I'll confess. As you know, wintery winds make me want to collect people. I guess that comes from my background, from being snowbound and lonely for days."

She told Carol that she'd coaxed Mrs. Prentiss into coming over to eat with them and watching a Thanksgiving special on television.

"How did you get her to consent? Especially tonight?" Carol asked.

"Well! It wasn't easy. She said the wind would do something or other to her sinuses. So I told her I'd back the car up the alley, right to her door."

"Can you?"

"Oh, yes, east-west lanes are open. The winds swept *them* almost clear," Nancy said.

"But there are six cups," Carol said.

"Yes. For Clea and Betty Rose," Nancy said. "It occurred to me that *you* needed company. So I called them. Clea has two new record albums. She wants to plan some sort of outing for tomorrow . . . if the wind ebbs . . . as the weatherman says it will."

"I doubt if there'll be any school," Carol said.

"There won't be," her mother said. "The superintendent issued a statement saying that it would be impossible for the township buses and the teachers who live outside the city to get here. Now I must get busy. Oh, one more thing. I asked Veronica. But they're having company."

"I know . . . the Weavers," Carol said. "I saw Corby go up the drive. In the wrecker."

"That's nice," Nancy said. "And as it should be."

Mrs. Prentiss was driven the half a block down the alley in time for supper. And the girls came afterward.

The girls watched the TV special with the adults then took their maple flavored treats and cups of warm cocoa to Carol's room. With Clea's records as background music, they planned a sledding party for the next afternoon. "We could never get all the snow off the pond with brooms," Betty Rose said. "It'd take a bulldozer or street sweeper."

They planned to ask Veronica and the Andrews twins. Then Clea said, "Why not call everyone within walking distance? No one will be able to get to this end of Randolph."

"Sally?" Betty asked. "Should we ask her?"

The girls looked at each other. It was Carol who spoke up and said, "We'd better. It would be unkind to leave her out." *But I don't think she'll come. Sledding would be kid stuff compared to the Nook.*

After the girls left, Carol wondered if they knew that Sally went to the dark and shadowy hangout. Probably so. Sally'd flaunt something like this, trying to prove something.

As Carol walked into her room, she caught a glimpse of headlights coming down the Kingsbury drive. Then she saw the wrecker in the lights from the gatepost globes. It was practically crawling through the piled up snow. A car would never make it.

She was ready to get into bed when Veronica called. The girls reviewed the hours since school was dismissed and Carol told Nicky about the sledding party.

"Are you all right up there?" Carol asked. "Plenty of food and everything?"

"Yes," Veronica said. "And Flora's on her feet and has taken over the cooking. But we're glad Bruce is in the cottage. Somehow we feel safer."

"He *did* get there then?" Carol asked.

"Yes. He came up a few minutes ago. Said he'd have to have snowshoes or a dog sled to get through

92

the drifts around the evergreen hedge." Veronica told Carol that he went around on the sidewalk and that was the way he got home. Going out of his way . . . finding streets clear enough for the truck. He'd come up to the big house to see if there was anything they needed.

Carol didn't float or drift into sleep that night. She dropped, or as her granddad would have said, she kerplunked into dreamland.

Sleep was a kind of feathery-and-cotton-wrapped-time until her dreams became filled with alarm. Bells and red lights and roaring motors were all mixed up in a kind of frightening roar. Carol woke herself up by turning over, back and forth.

Then she sat up. There *were* bells and red lights flashing on the snow . . . and sirens too! She ran to the window and saw a fire truck going around a bend in the Kingsbury drive. Fire! In *The Castle?*

Carol ran downstairs so fast that she tripped twice on the ruffle of her granny gown. Her mother was standing at the front window.

"Mom . . . what's. . . ."

"Don't worry, dear. Nothing's hurt . . . not much," Nancy said, "thanks to Bruce."

"But what. . . ."

"Come, sit down and I'll tell you . . . what I know."

Joanne Kingsbury had called a half an hour earlier asking if Tom Retherford could come up and help Bruce get the cars out of the garage. "That's where the fire was," Nancy said. "And snow was drifted against the doors."

"But how did it start? And who saw it?" Carol asked.

"I don't think they know how it started," Nancy said. "Not yet. But it was on the side next to the cottage on a kind of workbench under the window. The flames showed up on the snow. Bruce was going outside to start the nursery truck to let it run awhile. He'd done that every two hours all night, because of the cold."

"Did Mrs. Kingsbury tell you all this when she called for help?" Carol asked.

"No," Nancy said. "She called back when Bruce had the flames under control. I think it relieved her to talk."

"But I don't understand. If the fire is out, why is the engine going up the drive?"

"For a precaution," her mother said. "Your father and Bruce were afraid a spark might have fallen down inside the walls and might smolder and break out again."

"They sure weren't in any hurry," Carol said. "The firemen I mean."

"They couldn't be," Nancy explained. "A small county highway plow's ahead of them. The wind changed around midnight. Joanne said one drift on the bend was at least six feet high."

It was an hour before Tom Retherford came home. His boots were caked with snow and he spread three pairs of canvas work gloves on the hot register to dry.

Nancy had a pot of hot tea ready and made him a double-decker egg sandwich.

"That was a close call," Mr. Retherford said. "A few more minutes and the fire would have been out of control. The firemen couldn't have gotten there in time to save a thing."

"*That young man, Bruce, was pumping the fire extinguishers Veronica and her mother brought from all over the house,*" *Mr. Retherford said.*

"Did you see Veronica?" Carol asked.

"Yes. She was out there in the garage when I got there. That young man, Bruce, was pumping the fire extinguishers Veronica and her mother brought from all over the house."

"They're probably pretty scared," Nancy said.

"They were," Tom said. "Now they're grateful, mainly to Bruce — and that he was on the grounds."

Some of Mrs. Trent's words flashed into Carol's mind. "We can't do anyone's thinking for them or obey God for them."

Was this how good moved in the lives of people? Because Joanne had acted in a way that seemed good had she been protected on this cold and blizzardy night? Carol wasn't sure — not at all.

"Well! We *all* should be grateful for Bruce," Nancy said. "And so should Arthur Kingsbury, Jr."

14

The Retherfords went back to bed for a few hours of sleep. It was nine o'clock before Carol woke to see a glistening world.

The storm was over and sun was bright. Winchester was scultpured in white. Not a single track had been made on Randolph Street and those of the night before were erased in fluffiness.

Carol was surprised to see her father when she ran downstairs. "Aren't you going to the store?" she asked.

"Yes. After I read the paper, but I don't know why. There'll not be much business on a day like this."

"It's bad then?" Carol asked.

"Yes. Cars are stalled over on the Muncie Pike.

Some people took shelter in nearby farmhouses."

"Won't the snowplows clear the roads?" Carol asked.

"Yes, they're out now. There wasn't any use until the wind died down. But they can't get everywhere at once."

Nancy came to the door and said, "I just heard on the radio that a county snowplow is stuck in a drift at the edge of town."

After her father left on foot, Carol dressed in warm clothes and high boots and went across the alley. Nancy wanted to be sure Mrs. Prentiss was all right. Then she walked to the front of the house and wondered if she could get up the Kingsbury drive. *If I run into drifts I can detour around them.*

As soon as she walked through the big double doors, Carol felt a change in the atmosphere of the Kingsbury house. There was more laughter for one thing. It was coming from the kitchen. "Come on out," Nicky said. "We're making gingerbread men."

"Gingerbread men!"

"Yes. Mother's trimming trees in two of the hospital wards. We're baking and freezing ahead of time."

Flora was cutting the ginger-colored dough and putting the pans in the oven. Joanne was frosting bright-colored clothes on spicy cookies.

"I thought you'd be all upset . . .seeing about insurance or something," Carol said.

"Oh, on account of the fire, you mean," Joanne said. "Well, I called the agent. He can do whatever needs to be done. As for us . . . we're . . . what *are* we?"

"Happy," Veronica said.

"Grateful," Flora said. "Clear down to the tips of

our toes. We could've been burned out."

"Or up!" Joanne said. "If Bruce hadn't . . . I can't bear to think of what might have happened."

"Has he gone to work? Bruce, I mean."

"No. He came up to see if we were all right," Joanne said. "Now he's painting . . . or paying his rent as he puts it. For my future convalescent cottage."

Carol realized that this was a good time to tell about the idea she and Mrs. Trent had discussed. Mrs. Kingsbury was excited and pleased. "This would be the very best kind of help for these girls and boys. Caring people doing things for them. Do you think Mrs. Trent would have time to talk to me if I went over, when we get plowed out?"

Carol nodded and smiled. "She'd have time, even if she had to make time. She's a good listener."

The girls went to Nicky's room and within a few minutes Betty Rose called. Plans were made for the sledding party on Hiatt's Hill beyond the park. "We can't skate on snowdrifts," Carol said. "And sledding is all that's left around here."

They rounded up eleven other people who were told to hunt up sleds and wax the runners.

"I'd better go home and help Mom," Carol said. "She wants to make cinnamon rolls for us when we come in from whatever we planned. I'm supposed to vacuum the living room."

"Stay a little while, please," Nicky said. "I have this hunch or feeling. I need to talk to someone."

"What do you mean?" Carol asked.

"It's hard to put into words," Nicky said. "But I think last night's fire is a kind of turning point for us.

99

Mother's different. Like she used to be. Confident and positive. We've walked around on tiptoes for so long because of Father's anger. Now it's like Mother is making firm quick steps."

As Carol put on her boots, Veronica said, "Do you think we'll be plowed out today?"

"I doubt it," Carol said. "Unless there's some kind of emergency and this street would need to be open."

"Like last night," Veronica said. "It certainly drifted in quickly."

"Well, there's was a lot of snow and the wind was high," Carol said.

"Would you wait a minute?" Nicky said. "I'll walk part way with you."

As the two girls retraced Carol's tracks around the ridged drifts, Veronica said, "I've been thinking about something. Something I don't understand."

"What's that?" Carol asked.

"Well, you hear a lot on TV about drugs. About high schoolers and even younger kids using them. Once in awhile I hear parts of a conversation about it at school. But not from you or Betty or Clea. You seem to live . . . well, in a world apart."

Carol stopped in a cleared place in front of the greenhouse. The windows were steamy but not frosted. She saw glimpses of color — pink, lavender, and yellow in the heated glass-enclosed shelter.

"I guess you're right," she said. "We do move in our own path. By choice. Oh, we know about drugs and could name some kids who use them. A few anyway." She thought of Sally Blane and hoped she wouldn't be on the list.

"But you're not bothered by this?" Nicky asked.

"Well, yes. Not for myself. My parents have set up rules that are kind of a shelter. But for others. I mean it's scary to think someone who sits next to you in class may be harming herself. But as Mrs. Trent says, I can't do anyone else's obeying. And my mother says we all must find our own secret place."

The girls were near the gate when Veronica said, "Do you know something? I feel better. I'm not the only one who's had to live by rules."

"No," Carol said. "But you have been restricted more than I have. I wouldn't want to live without rules. I'd feel unanchored if I could do everything I wanted. Well! I'll see you at my house at three."

Within a half hour after the young people and the sleds congregated on Hiatt's Hill, a hard packed track ran down one side away from the drifts.

One of the Andrews twins had a four-man toboggan and three trips on it gave the snow track a smooth and glistening surface.

The sun came out from behind the veil of smoky gray clouds at intervals. Someone built a fire at the foot of the hill with dead and fallen limbs. Numb toes were warmed back to life, then chilled again. Cheeks were red, eyes bright, and voices happy-toned until Carol looked down from the top of the slope and saw Bruce Harrison walking from the direction of *The Castle. Something's wrong! I just know it.* She looked aroung for Veronica, then remembered. Her friend was next to the last person on the long sled which was halfway down the slope.

Carol felt a strong urge to be near Nicky when Bruce reached the hill. She grabbed a small child's coaster and began a bouncing descent.

Veronica had seen Bruce and was hurrying to meet him. When Carol was within hearing distance she heard Bruce say. "It *may* not be as bad as it sounds." He was holding Nicky's mittened hands and she was shaking her head back and forth saying, "No, no, no." The pink pom-pom on her knitted tam bounced.

Carol walked over and touched Nicky's elbow and she saw the clouded look in the violet eyes. "Oh, Carol. My father's plane is lost. Somewhere in Colorado."

Bruce said, "That's right, Carol. The news came over the television station in Indianapolis. And bulletins keep being repeated on the radio station here."

"I must go home," Veronica said, "to Mother. Is she. . . ."

"She's all right," Bruce said. "She came down and asked me to tell you. She's calling the airlines now for direct news."

"Would you go home with me, Carol?" Veronica asked. "I hate to spoil. . . ."

"I wouldn't stay. Not now," Carol said.

"I'll go tell the others why you're leaving." Bruce said. "And I'll be near if there's anything to do."

"You couldn't get away could you?" Carol asked.

"Oh, yes. The state highway plows came down Randolph Street as I left. Someone from the glass plant must have asked them to open the street."

As the girls hurried west, Nicky said, "Plowing out the street won't help. Daddy's out there some place. Maybe in the mountains. Maybe hurt. Maybe even.

Oh, Carol, this isn't the way things should end. With a big gap between us. With him so bitter."

"Oh, Carol," Nicky said, "my father's plane is lost somewhere in Colorado."

Carol put her arm around Veronica. "Don't give up. You don't know that he isn't all right."

"You're right," Nicky said. "I musn't make things harder for Mother either." They were within a block and a half of the stone entrance. "That's Alexandra," Veronica said. "She's come home. That's one good thing about having the street opened."

15

A kind of cloud hung over the small city of Winchester for the next two days. Anxiety was spread and intensified by the frequent news bulletins announcing that no trace had been found of the missing plane. People seemed to be hushed and listening, waiting for news.

Nancy Retherford spoke of this attitude when she came back from a shopping trip the second evening after the plane from California was reported missing. "People are wonderful sometimes," she said as she hung her coat in the closet under the stairs. "Very few people really knew Mr. Kingsbury. And he's never been warm or friendly. But there's a concern in people's conversation. A worried look on their faces."

"I know," Carol said. "Kids at school talk a lot about it. Even those from the townships."

"The buses did make it today then?" Nancy asked.

"Yes. One was half an hour late. The one that comes over the winding Hillsboro road. What'd you buy up town?" Carol asked.

"This is no-question season," Nancy said. "Remember?"

"Oh," Carol said. "You mean you've started Christmas shopping already! Even before Thanksgiving!"

"Well. You know me! Snowy weather puts me in the mood. And we may not have much of this weather in December. But I did feel a little guilty . . . having joyous and gay feelings when there's so much trouble in the world, like in the Kingsbury family. Have you talked to Veronica?"

"No," Carol said. "But I think I'll go up after awhile. She asked me to bring her assignments and a couple of books."

"I think I'll go along if it's all right with you," her mother said. "I can't *do* anything. But the country in me says, 'Be neighborly.' "

Joanne met them at the door. She was holding the Little Weaver in her arms. "Come in," she said. "We need someone besides ourselves and the telephone."

"Have the calls bothered you?" Nancy asked.

"Yes, they have," Joanne said. "Mainly because we hope each one brings us news . . . good, naturally, and we don't want the line to be busy. But so far. . . ."

Alexandra and Veronica came down the wide, curving staircase. They all went into the library and Carol and her mother stayed for nearly an hour. Everyone succeeded in sounding fairly casual for the benefit of the others. But the undercurrent of strain was real and strong.

As the Retherfords left, Joanne said, "No matter what we say or do all kinds of frightening pictures go through our minds."

"And questions," Alexandra said. "Like, why can't they find them, and are they really trying?"

The unspoken questions were answered later that night. Carol had gone to bed when her mother called from the foot of the stairs. "They've found the plane. Veronica's father is alive. There's a special report on the late news."

Carol hurried down in time to see the news pictures of the wrecked plane on the snowy, lower slope of a mountain. Another showed two men, on stretchers, being loaded into an ambulance.

"They're hurt then," Carol said.

"Not much," Nancy said. "The pilot has a broken arm and contusions. And Mr. Kingsbury a fractured ankle and cuts. But they've been out there in the snow two days. That couldn't have been good for them."

The newcast ended with the report that both men were being treated in the hospital in Boulder, Colorado.

"Well, a lot of people will sleep easier tonight," Carol's father said, "besides the people in *The Castle*."

"I wonder why there's been so much concern," Nancy said. "I mean since Mr. Kingsbury's not especially well-liked."

"That's true," Tom said. "But he *is* respected. You know there's been no serious labor problems at Kingsbury Industries. He's a fair man. A lot of people depend on his plant for making their living."

"But that's selfish. Wanting him to be alive for their good," Nancy said.

Tom smiled and said, "Honey, you know people! There are all kinds of thinking and feeling. And I'm sure some are genuine and human in not wanting tragedy to strike the Kingsburys."

As he spoke the doorbell rang and Nancy opened it for Nicky, who was smiling radiantly.

"Corby brought me down," she said. "He's going home to get more clothes for the baby. But I just had to tell you. Daddy called. From the hospital."

"And he's not hurt badly?" Carol said.

"No. And he's being flown to Indianapolis tomorrow. He'll be home about noon. Mother and Corby are going to meet him."

The Retherfords looked at each other in surprise. "Corby?" Nancy said.

"Yes. That's part of what's so wonderful. Daddy talked to all of us . . . except the baby who was asleep. Mother, Flora, and I first. But when Mother told him that Alexandra was there he didn't say anything for what seemed like *ages*. We all watched Mother's face. Then tears began to roll as the most beautiful smile came . . . like a glowing light . . . and she turned and said, "Your father wants to talk to you, Alexandra."

Nicky told the Retherfords that her sister couldn't say much and neither could their father. But after a few minutes Alexandra looked up at her husband and said, "Daddy wants to be introduced to you."

"You can't believe the change in our house," Nicky said. "Mother called the boys and they're all flying home . . . will be here tomorrow night. Flora is in the kitchen making hot-water pie crust."

"Pie crust!" Nancy said. "It's after eleven o'clock,"

"I *know*," Veronica said. "But no one up there cares. Flora said that Mr. Arthur hadn't really relished her strawberry pies in a couple of months of Sundays. And maybe now he will. So she aims to have some on hand when he gets home. Mother and Alexandra are putting fresh linen in the boys' room. I doubt if anyone will sleep much tonight."

After Corby Weaver picked Nicky up, Nancy said, "I wonder if Joanne, or any of the others told Mr. Kingsbury about the fire?"

That question was answered late the next afternoon. Carol had seen two cars coming down the driveway as she walked home from school and thought, "They'll probably have a lot of visitors. I'll not bother Nicky."

But she found a message from her mother. "Am at the church sewing. Veronica wants you to go up and meet her father."

Carol brushed her hair and put on a fresh white blouse under her bittersweet jumper. Her heart fluttered as she rang the doorbell. Years of standing in awe of Mr. Kingsbury made her dread this meeting.

Alexandra met her at the door. "Nicky . . . meant to meet you. But she's upstairs bringing the baby down from his nap. Here, let me have your coat."

"I noticed something. Do you call Veronica Nicky now?" Carol asked.

"Yes. I like it. It fits. Come on . . . Oh, there you are, Nicky! I'll take this young man and you can take Carol into the library."

The first thought that came to Carol as she walked into the room was, *He's so handsome, so incredibly good-looking.* It seemed strange that she hadn't noticed this before. But she'd never seen Mr. Kingsbury up close before except in a car — a long car that glided by before she could get a good look.

"Daddy," Nicky said. "This is Carol Retherford."

The tall man with salt-and-pepper hair started to rise from the deep leather chair. Then he smiled and said, "I can't be courteous with a cast on my ankle. But it's good to meet you." Then as Carol walked to the fanning half-circle of the firelight, he added, "Of course! You *are* the one I've noticed. You're the best roller skater on Randolph Street. I've seen you sail over the hump made by roots of the big sycamore tree at the corner."

"Well, that took practice," Carol said. "I'm glad you are safe, sir. And home."

"So am I," Mr. Kingsbury said. "So am I."

Joanne came into the room. Her lovely face looked years younger. The strain was eased.

Nicky took Carol into the sun-room and told her more of what had happened in the last few hours. "We all thought Daddy would be exhausted, that he'd have to go to bed. But he wouldn't. He wanted to hear what had happened here. So we told him. Everything."

"About Bruce?" Carol asked.

"And the fire." Veronica said. "And that led into the subject of Mother's home for children."

110

"And he wasn't angry?"

"No," Veronica answered. "He said that the hours in the snow had given him time to think and to analyze his own actions. 'Somehow the hours of cold warmed my heart, thawed my stubborn pride!' is the way he put it. In fact he's been figuring on how much it would cost to add a playroom to the cottage."

"Has he met Bruce?" Carol asked.

"Not yet," Nicky said. "He's at work. But I didn't tell you, did I? Something good has come *his* way too. He's going to work for Corby. They talked this over last night before the good news came. It'll be a better paying job. And there's a place to live above the new station. A room and kitchenette and bath next to the storeroom for tires and stuff."

Carol shook her head. "It's hard to believe that things have changed so much in a few hours."

"I know," Veronica said. "It's like . . . sunrise after a long, long night."

"Do you think your father will allow you to have dates with Bruce?"

"Probably," Veronica said. "But I'm not going to rush things by asking. I'd feel greedy. So much good has come to us. I feel that I've moved into a new world. Or is it that I'm living in it for the first time?"

As Carol walked toward home the lights came on at the gateposts and began to glow. She turned and looked back at the white brick home. Nearly every window was a golden rectangle in the gray-blue light of dusk. Somehow Carol knew she'd never again call Veronica's home *The Castle*.

The Author

Dorothy Hamilton was born in Delaware County, Indiana, where she still lives. She received her elementary and secondary education in the schools of Cowan and Muncie, Indiana. She attended Ball State University, Muncie, and has taken work by correspondence from Indiana University, Bloomington, Indiana. She has attended professional writing courses, first as a student and later as an instructor.

Mrs. Hamilton grew up in the Methodist Church and participated in numerous school, community, and church activities until the youngest of her seven children was married.

Then she felt led to become a private tutor. This service has become a mission of love. Several hundred girls and boys have come to Mrs. Hamilton for gentle encouragement, for renewal of self-esteem, and to learn to work.

The experiences of motherhood and tutoring have inspired Mrs. Hamilton in much of her writing.

Seven of her short stories have appeared in quarterlies and one was nominated for the American Literary Anthology. Since 1967 she has had fifty serials published, more than four dozen short stories, and several articles in religious magazines. She has also written for radio and newspapers.

Mrs. Hamilton is author of *Anita's Choice, Christmas for Holly, Charco, The Killdeer, Tony Savala, Jim Musco, Settled Furrows, Kerry, The Blue Caboose, Mindy, The Quail, Jason, The Gift of a Home, The Eagle, Cricket, Neva's Patchwork Pillow, The Castle,* and *Linda's Raintree.*